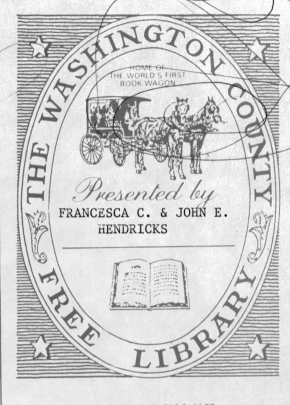

DECORATING
WITH FLOWERS

DECORATING
WITH FLOWERS

Jenny Raworth & Susan Berry

PHOTOGRAPHY BY MIKE NEWTON

COLLINS & BROWN

DECORATING WITH FLOWERS

First published in Great Britain in 1999 by
COLLINS & BROWN LIMITED, London House,
Great Eastern Wharf, Parkgate Road, London SW11 4NQ

Distributed in the United States and Canada by
Sterling Publishing Co, 387 Park Avenue South,
New York, NY 10016, USA

Copyright © Collins & Brown Limited 1999
Text copyright © Jenny Raworth and Susan Berry 1999
Photography copyright © Collins & Brown Limited 1999

The right of Jenny Raworth and Susan Berry to be
identified as the authors of this work has been asserted
by them in accordance with the Copyright, Designs
and Patents Act, 1988.

British Library Cataloguing-in-Publication Data:
A catalogue record for this book is available from
the British Library.

ISBN 1 85585 460 0 (hardback edition)
ISBN 1 85585 644 1 (paperback edition)

Conceived, edited and designed for Collins & Brown by
PHOEBUS EDITIONS LTD, City House, 72-80 Leather Lane,
London EC1N 7TR.

Designer Debbie Mole
Editor Theresa Donaghey
Photography Mike Newton

Reproduction by Hong Kong Graphic and Printing Ltd
Printed and bound in Singapore by Tien Wah

CAUTION
*Publisher's note: Burning candles form a part of the decorations in this
book, however, they are of course a fire hazard and must be treated
with caution at all times. Always consider safety when lighting a
candle and never leave burning candles unattended at any time.*

5 2 3   5 8 6 2

CONTENTS

MATCHING SETTINGS
& DISPLAYS 10

SITUATIONS FOR
FLOWERS 28

INTRODUCTION

FLOWERS BRING A HOUSE or apartment to life. No matter how well decorated your home may be, it may lack charm without the addition of some form of floral decoration. In days gone by, housewives were trained in the art of flower arranging as an essential household skill, and gardens were organized to produce flowers to cut for the house.

While the lifestyle of most people today makes this impossible, there is an ever greater need to create an attractive and soothing atmosphere at home as the pressures of daily life increase. You can do this successfully, and simply, using a variety of floral material – fresh flowers, pot-grown plants, dried flowers and even artificial flowers – so that there is something to bring vibrancy and interest to your house at all times of the year.

A simple and effective summer jug of fresh peonies.

▲ **BEFORE**
A fireplace is often the focal point in a room. Without a fire burning, the room can feel noticeably empty.

► **AFTER**
The fireplace, filled with a generous display of large dried and artificial flowers, is now transformed into a stunning centrepiece to the room. Instructions for this arrangement are given on pages 64-5.

MATCHING FLOWERS TO SETTING

Decoration style is very individual and often reflects the home owner's personality and taste. If flower arrangements and decorations are to work well, and harmonize with the setting, they, too, must be created and conceived in an individual way, using flower types, colours and textures that blend seamlessly with their surroundings. New ideas in flower arranging allow you to be both creative and original, using strong colour contrasts, bold leaf shapes, and striking containers in displays which are a far cry from the distorted and frequently lifeless 'arrangements' that used to win prizes at village fetes!

Autumn windfall flowers in a glass container.

▲ **BEFORE**
A desk or cabinet in a corner of a room would benefit greatly from a simple, generous display of fresh or dried flowers.

▶ **AFTER**
A jug of garden roses (see pages 104-106), softened with sprigs of lady's mantle, brings this corner to life. A dried lavender basket would be just as effective (see pages 101-103).

In most houses and apartments, there are particular places – small focal points – where a flowering or plant display is most effective. These tend to be on table centres, in fireplaces, on shelves, in the hall or on the landing, or perhaps in a window recess. By far the most successful arrangements are those that are designed with the space they are to fill already in mind. A professional flower arranger will always visit the situation in which the arrangement is to be positioned, and design the arrangement accordingly, and this simple premise works just as well at home, too.

Firstly, flower and foliage colours and textures should be in keeping with the setting, either harmonizing or contrasting (see pages 12-17).

Winter-flowering heathers
in a painted tin.

◄ **FRESH FLOWERS**
Symmetry, texture and a carefully chosen colour palette play an important part in creating impact with fresh flowers – you do not need elaborate blooms as this chrysanthemum, agapanthus and viburnum table setting amply demonstrates.

► **DRIED FLOWERS**
Equally simple in construction, but strikingly different in its impact, this wreath of dried yellow flax seeds is nevertheless eye-catching and almost sculptural in form.

Autumn sloe berries informally arranged in a glass jar.

Delicate glasses filled with, for example, tiny scented narcissus, would complement a range of yellow china; bright orange gerberas set in brilliant blue pots could line up along the window-sill of a minimalist apartment to give an otherwise plain room a splash of vibrant colour. Containers should also be chosen to complement the style of the surroundings, and the scale and form of the space they are to fill. A tall terracotta vase, with a similarly tall and elegant display of twisted willow branches, is ideal for a narrow bleached oak table in a modern-style hall; a wide, shallow silver bowl filled with garden roses makes an ideal table centre in a period setting.

NEW IDEAS

Everyone has favourite colours and flowers but half the fun of flower arranging lies in being open to new ways of arranging flowers. Try putting together unusual or striking colour combinations; find or make your own interesting containers, and keep an eye open for different forms of flower or foliage. The newly available exquisitely coloured artificial flowers, almost indistinguishable from the real thing, are a far cry from the inelegant and unrealistic *faux* flowers of yesteryear, and can make a wonderful permanent arrangement in an otherwise inhospitable situation – like a hot sunny window (see page 30). Containers do not have to be bought expressly for flowers. You can use any number of

Scented spring flowers in a china bowl.

◄ POT PLANTS
A few container-grown Dutch hyacinths are transformed into an impressive arrangement with a practical pussy willow support and a base of moss, ivy and fungus. It has the added benefit of lasting longer than a fresh arrangement, too.

► ARTIFICIAL FLOWERS
Man-made flowers can be deceptively realistic and are an ideal solution for a permanent display in a window, where fresh flowers would quickly fade or die.

Enliven artificial flowers, like these silk tulips, with fresh foliage.

imaginative containers for flower arrangements, from a cracked mug or teapot to tin cans covered in moss or leaves. The art then lies in marrying the flowers and containers together to maximum advantage – for example, a little posy of wildflowers in a home-made mossy pot or half-a-dozen Victorian clay pots of auricula primroses in a wire milk-bottle container. On a rather grander scale, a hand-painted bucket filled with long-stemmed large-headed flowers will fill a summer fireplace.

The aim of this book is to start you thinking creatively about the places in which you can display flowers, and the ways in which you choose to display them, using every imaginable kind of floral material.

Matching
settings &
DISPLAYS

Choosing an appropriate style of arrangement, and of container, for the setting is the key to effective floral decoration. In this chapter, the forms, colours and textures of fresh and dried flowers, and the different kinds of container, are examined in the context of their setting.

CHOOSING COLOURS
Neutrals and Earth Tones

I T IS IMPORTANT when choosing flowers – whether fresh or dried – for a room to pick colours and textures that are appropriate for the setting. The suggestions shown on these pages are by no means comprehensive, but they will help to give you some idea of how to achieve a harmonious balance of colour, texture and mood for different settings. You need to look not only at the colour of the flowers, but at the form they take – whether stiff and upright, or gracefully branching and arching – and the texture, size and form of any foliage – glossy or matt, spiny or soft, large or small, held in upright spires or twining and loose.

Neutral shades are among the most popular in the decorator's palette as they are timeless and very easy to live with. Soft pale shades allow you plenty of scope with decoration, both in the colours of furnishings and in the more ephemeral flowers that you choose. Cool white and cream or green flower arrangements work very well with quite sophisticated white and black contrasts; soft creams, beiges and peach shades look good in the faded chintz interiors so redolent of English country houses, while with the deeper earth-toned neutrals of terracotta and brick you can use soft and subtly shaded autumnal berries and seedheads, as well as grasses, to great effect.

◄ CREAM AND WHITE TONES
Sophisticated monochromatic settings – dining rooms or table centres with white damask cloths and pale china – make an ideal showplace for white and green arrangements, using sophisticated flowers such as lilies, freesias or white florist's roses, with darker foliage to offset the pale colours of the flowers.

sea holly
(ERYNGIUM)

Easter lily
(LILIUM LONGIFLORUM)

september flower
(ASTER sp.)

Freesia

Eucalyptus

Hypericum

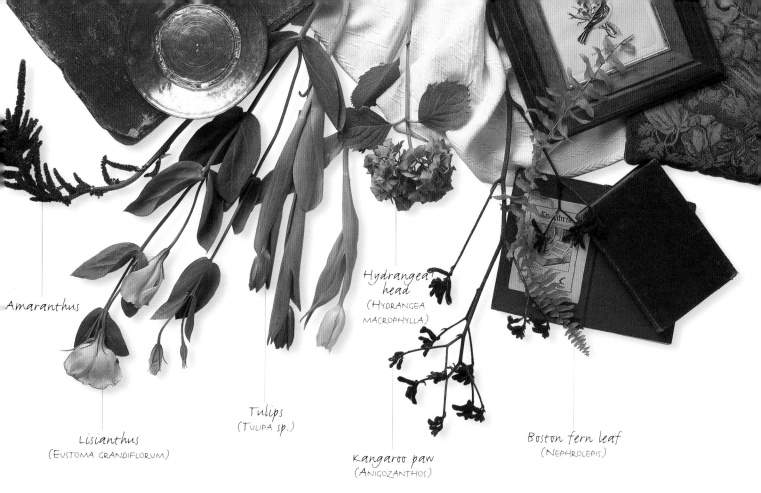

Amaranthus

Hydrangea head
(HYDRANGEA MACROPHYLLA)

Lisianthus
(EUSTOMA GRANDIFLORUM)

Tulips
(TULIPA sp.)

Kangaroo paw
(ANIGOZANTHOS)

Boston fern leaf
(NEPHROLEPIS)

▲ **BEIGE AND PEACH TONES**

Soft natural wood, leather and stone and creamy coloured fabrics make an ideal setting for delicate pale-toned flowers, contrasted with some deeper pinks and reds to give an overall warm, glowing effect for a drawing room, study or hallway.

▼ **TERRACOTTA AND EARTH TONES**

Strong shapes and rich colours look good in settings like these, often favoured for kitchens and halls. Autumnal fresh flowers come in a range of suitable golds, russets and reddish browns, or dried flowers such as chrysanthemums and achilleas could be used instead. Textural arrangements of wheat and barley would go well with this kind of setting.

Chrysanthemum

sunflower
(HELIANTHUS)

Alstroemeria

Pyracantha

Crab apples
(MALUS sp.)

Ivy
(HEDERA HELIX 'Goldheart')

Vibrant Brights

FOR MORE MODERN, sharp-looking interiors, with clear colours and strong shapes, you can choose flower arrangements with contrasts of bright colours, either in mixed displays of contrasting colours, or perhaps by using a grouped display of yellow tulips with a pot of bright red gerberas, lilies and tulips next to them, perhaps the yellow tulips in a scarlet container, and the scarlet arrangement in a yellow one. Warm colours such as bright yellows, reds and oranges can also be used effectively in white or neutral interiors to create

a welcome single splash of strong colour. Large waxy flowers – lilies, tulips, amaryllis and hyacinths – are excellent for this purpose.

Sharp acid contrasts of bright yellows, apple greens and brilliant blues look good with jewel-coloured glass, sharp gingham or canvas deckchair stripes, and expanses of plain coloured sailcloth. Glass containers will help to emphasize the strength of colour of the flowers, as will simple containers in a plain contrasting colour.

Mimosa
(ACACIA DEALBATA)

Lily
(LILIUM *sp.*)

Freesia

Carnation
(DIANTHUS *sp.*)

Ivy
(HEDERA *sp.*)

Tulip
(TULIPA *sp.*)

Gerbera

◄ **YELLOW AND RED**
Rich warm yellows and reds combine to create vibrant colour contrasts, ideally using blocks of colour. Large-headed blooms such as gerberas make a dramatic impact. Waxy petals, such as those of tulips, catch the light and enhance depth of colour.

Gerbera

Narcissus
(NARCISSUS
'soleil d'Or')

Tulip
(TULIPA sp.)

Button
chrysanthemum

Safflower
(CARTHAMUS)

▲ TURQUOISE AND LIME

*A cooler palette of equally vibrant colours
using acid greens, sharp yellows, strong
blues and oranges can be used in a modern
setting to great effect, either in small posies
or jugs of single-colour themed flowers –
little formal pots of narcissi, yellow tulips
cut down into a wide trug or massed heads
of chrysanthemums in bright burnt orange,
coupled with grass-green foliage displays.*

▼ BRIGHT BLUE

*Clear, strong blues can be used as a straightforward contrast with white. Flowers with a
well-defined form and large flowerheads, like irises, anemones or hyacinths, make a bold
statement in this kind of setting. Use bright blue Dutch irises with a little apple-green foliage
in a white china jug for maximum effect. Make sure the container has a simple form; fussy
patterns and indeterminate shapes distract the eye. Fresh mid-greens harmonize well
with mid-blues for a more subtle, but equally fresh look. Minor touches of yellow or bright
red serve to underline the colour contrast.*

Dried larkspur
(CONSOLIDA sp.)

sea holly
(ERYNGIUM)

Dutch iris
(IRIS RETICULATA)

Hyacinth
(HYACINTHUS)

Polyanthus
(PRIMULA sp.)

Magnolia leaves
(MAGNOLIA
GRANDIFLORA)

Anemone

Gerbera

Harmonizing Colourways

FOR MANY PEOPLE, soft harmonizing colour schemes in pale pinks, mauves, powder blues and white epitomize the main delights of flowers in the house, and certainly these colours work extremely well with the interior style known as 'English country house' in which faded chintz forms the leitmotiv of the decoration. Softly harmonizing flower colours can also work well in the more autumnal colours of soft yellows, rusts and pale greens in neutral, pale green, gold or terracotta rooms.

Generally speaking, the seasons determine these softly harmonizing displays, with the pinks and blues predominating in summer, and the more golden russet tones in autumn.

Delicate china containers with subtle figurative patterns, polished silver or pewter and crystal work particularly well with these informal arrangements in which a variety of foliage and flowers are combined in loosely constructed displays.

Foliage can be used to soften the display – feathery ferns, soft lady's mantle leaves or trailing ivy will all help to create a more gentle 'country' look to the arrangement. Equally, 'hedgerow' flowers, with their small flowers and soft colours are ideal.

▼ BLUES, MAUVES AND PINKS
Colours in this harmonizing range in the 'warm' part of the spectrum are ideal for welcoming, cosy rooms, particularly sitting rooms or bedrooms where there is plenty of fabric. Pale creams can be used to lighten and soften arrangements. There are many dried flowers in this colour range, particularly lavender, roses and peonies, their muted colours blending well with chintz and floral fabrics.

Aster

Lisianthus
(EUSTOMA GRANDIFLORUM)

Lavender
(LAVANDULA SP.)

Broom
(GENISTA)

Pussy willow
(SALIX CAPREA)

Rose
(ROSA SP.)

Orchid
(CYMBIDIUM)

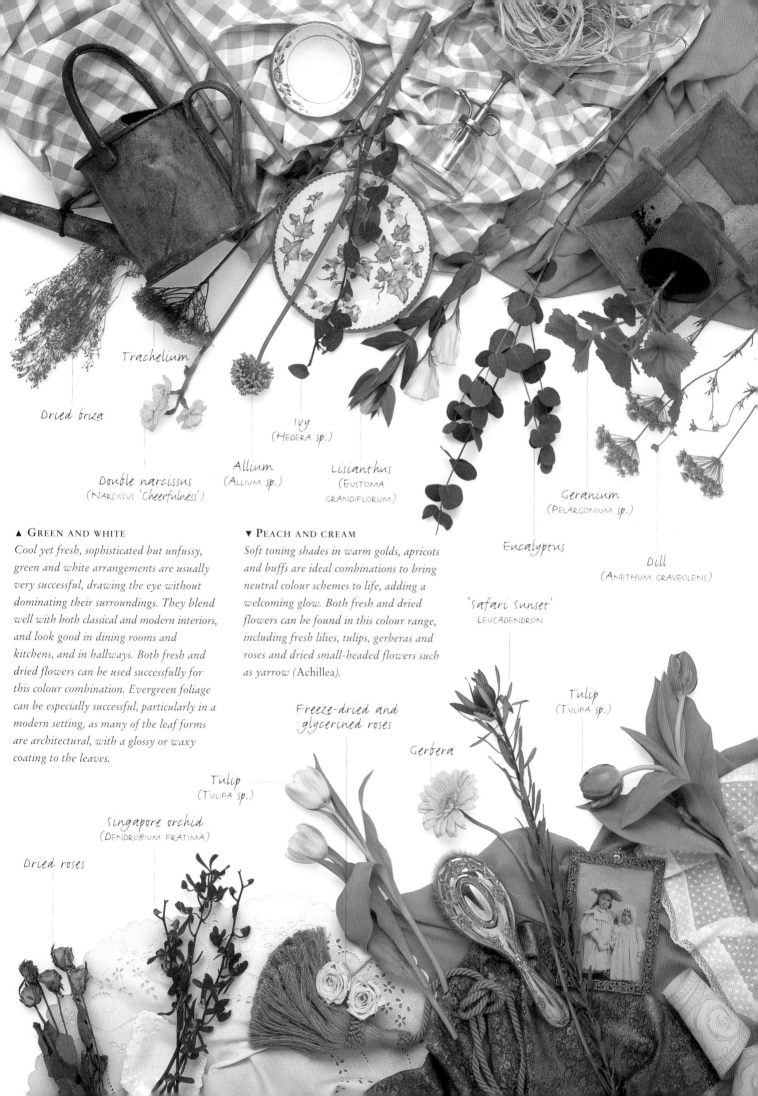

Trachelium

Dried briza

Ivy
(HEDERA sp.)

Double narcissus
(NARCISSUS 'Cheerfulness')

Allium
(ALLIUM sp.)

Lisianthus
(EUSTOMA
GRANDIFLORUM)

Geranium
(PELARGONIUM sp.)

Eucalyptus

Dill
(ANETHUM GRAVEOLENS)

▲ GREEN AND WHITE

*Cool yet fresh, sophisticated but unfussy,
green and white arrangements are usually
very successful, drawing the eye without
dominating their surroundings. They blend
well with both classical and modern interiors,
and look good in dining rooms and
kitchens, and in hallways. Both fresh and
dried flowers can be used successfully for
this colour combination. Evergreen foliage
can be especially successful, particularly in a
modern setting, as many of the leaf forms
are architectural, with a glossy or waxy
coating to the leaves.*

▼ PEACH AND CREAM

*Soft toning shades in warm golds, apricots
and buffs are ideal combinations to bring
neutral colour schemes to life, adding a
welcoming glow. Both fresh and dried
flowers can be found in this colour range,
including fresh lilies, tulips, gerberas and
roses and dried small-headed flowers such
as yarrow (Achillea).*

'safari sunset'
LEUCADENDRON

Freeze-dried and
glycerined roses

Gerbera

Tulip
(TULIPA sp.)

Tulip
(TULIPA sp.)

Singapore orchid
(DENDROBIUM FRATIMA)

Dried roses

CONTAINERS

General Information

THE CONTAINER IS the key to the success of the arrangement. It must complement the flowers or foliage in texture, colour and form and enhance the display without dominating it. When you arrange flowers for your house, you sometimes look for a suitable container in which to put flowers you have bought or been given, or, more often if you grow your own flowers, you have a favourite container which stands in a permanent position, and which you aim to keep filled, when you can, with seasonal material.

It is very easy to become complacent and conventional about the containers you use without realizing how the impact of different containers can vary. These pages show some of the choices open to you, including both antique and modern containers in a variety of different materials. Try to be adventurous in your choice, and keep your eyes open for chipped or broken bargains – jugs, dishes and bowls – that can be bought inexpensively because of their condition and whose faults and blemishes are often easily masked by their contents.

Enamelled jug

Tin vase

Enamelled pail

Tin can

Tin jug

Tin plant pots

Bread tin

Aluminium, Tin and Wirework

METAL AND WIREWORK containers have the virtue that they are monochromatic, allowing the flower shape and colour to dictate the mood of the display. Solid metal containers can be used either to create a strong statement of form, matched to an architectural display of tulips, for example, or they can be used as the contrast to a much more ethereal arrangement – massed tiny heads of gypsophila, cow parsley or field buttercups for example (see page 39).

Many different kinds of metal can be used – silver, aluminium and plain honest tin. They come in many forms – from buckets and jugs to household tins and pots. The metal can be unadorned, or enamelled or painted. Shiny metal suits strong displays while dull and beaten metal looks well with pale colours and delicate textures. Even household baking tins make good containers, as do recycled tins. These types of container are ideal for displays of fresh flowers in a natural arrangement.

First introduced in the nineteenth century, wire containers are back in vogue again. Particularly good for holding displays of container-grown plants, they can also be used, with the help of moss and a waterproof, invisible inner container, for fresh flowers. They look best containing small pots of violas or ferns, to echo the Victorian charm of their early forebears.

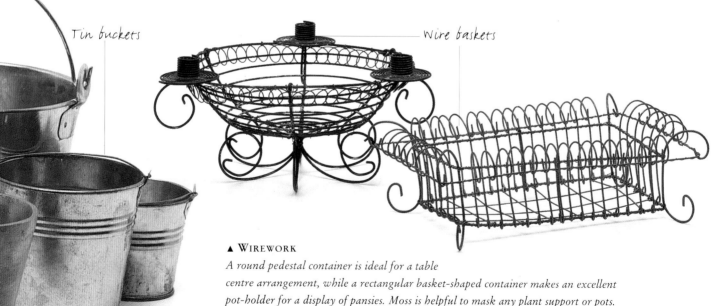

Tin buckets

Wire baskets

Terracotta pot painted silver

▲ **WIREWORK**
A round pedestal container is ideal for a table centre arrangement, while a rectangular basket-shaped container makes an excellent pot-holder for a display of pansies. Moss is helpful to mask any plant support or pots.

◄ **ALUMINIUM AND TIN**
Metal containers, whether brilliantly polished, enamelled or matt in texture, have a pleasantly smooth and plain appearance which can be used to great effect to provide a base for an arrangement which emphasizes the beauty of the flowers and foliage. Buckets, jugs, bowls and even recycled tin cans make useful containers that can be used in distinctive and varied ways – strikingly modern, period-style or cottage garden.

Glazed earthenware
storage jar

Earthenware
jug

Terracotta
bowl

Terracotta
pots

Ceramic jugs

▲ Terracotta

Terracotta has a richness of colour and simplicity of form that makes it an ideal foil for a wide range of flower displays, from massed bunches of dried flowers and herbs, to bright displays of single-colour themed flowers. Smaller terracotta pots can be lined up along a window-sill or shelf to create an attractive repeating arrangement, filled with single flowers or bunches of dried lavender or marjoram. More ornate pots can be used unfilled in a grouped display to add architectural interest.

▶ Ceramic

With their rough texture and simple outlines, earthenware jugs and pots are the ideal containers for a modern house or for a kitchen arrangement. Bright, bold flowers are ideal, as are berries and seedheads in autumn. Simple, single arrangements of pansies, primulas and domes of dried roses are also brilliantly displayed in these kinds of container. Although only a tiny selection of the china that you could use for containers is shown here, it gives you an idea of the range of forms, colours, shapes and sizes at your disposal, from a sauceboat dish to an old ginger jar, and from modern china vases to simple milk jugs.

Ginger jar

Ceramics and Terracotta

THE TRADITIONAL MATERIALS for containers – plain, glazed, decorated or in their natural state – ceramics, earthenware and terracotta make a splendidly diverse range to suit almost every kind of display. The myriad shapes – bowls, jugs, cups, mugs, jars and plates – allow you great scope as a flower arranger. They are also the most versatile and work well for dried, fresh or artificial forms of flower material. Earthenware tends to be best suited to simple colours and flower forms and shapes, its rough texture and clear form an ideal companion for them. Fine china with restrained patterning makes a suitable container for pretty fresh flowers with delicate forms and pastel colours, and for dried flowers as well.

Household cups and mugs can be used for simple arrangements such as a single bunch of dried flowers. They look effective if you arrange a row of them in among your china collection. Larger pots, tureens and vegetable dishes can be used for handsome flower arrangements for table centres.

Ceramic vases

Tea caddy

Cream jar

Ceramic jar

sauce boat

Ceramic pot

Glass

Baskets and Wood

MOST FORMS OF glass container are see-through, although there is a growing range of modern 'smoked' or opaque glass, some of it in wonderfully rich colours. The advantage of a clear glass container is that your eye focuses entirely on its contents, rather than on its form. It is therefore an ideal type to use to show off particularly glorious flowers. However, because the stems and water show through you need to be meticulous about clearing the stems of leaves and replacing the water (see page 117).

SIMPLE COUNTRY-STYLE baskets in woven rush and cane are invaluable containers for a wide range of flower types, but in particular for dried flowers and for pot-grown ones. You can keep a range of them on top of a kitchen cupboard, filled with some of your own dried flowers (see page 59). Remember that when you want to use them for pot-grown or fresh flowers, you will have to provide an inner, waterproof sleeve (an old black plastic bin liner, cut down to size, is ideal). Moss is very useful for hiding the liner.

► **CLEAR GLASS**
Adaptable and versatile, clear glass containers fit well into any setting and can be used, depending on their form, with a wide range of arrangements – dramatic displays, elegant groupings or simple posies. The transparent quality of glass gives predominance to the arrangement and makes it suitable for window settings and cool, light rooms. Well-prepared green stems can look attractive through the glass and decorative materials, such as marbles, can be used to anchor flowers for added impact.

Old wooden sieve

Woven wicker baskets

Wooden trug

▲ WOVEN BASKETS, BOXES AND TRUGS

The rustic associations of wood and wicker lend themselves to natural-looking dried flower arrangements such as aromatic stalks of lavender. Pots of spring bulbs look effective, as do posies of cottage garden flowers; both need an inner watertight lining or container.

▼ COLOURED GLASS

Modern, streamlined shapes combined with opaque brightly coloured glass create excellent containers for displays of just a few eye-catching flowers or shrubs with strong simple shapes. Opaque glass is a good choice for modern settings but it is not ideal, generally speaking, for dried flowers which would be overwhelmed by its sharp colours and outlines.

Coloured glass vases

Plain glass vases

DECORATING CONTAINERS

Verdigris Florist's Bucket

INEXPENSIVE METAL OR terracotta containers can be painted for a more colourful, interesting appearance, or to tone in with a particular flower arrangement that you have in mind. This little florist's bucket was given an antiqued verdigris effect very simply by using three shades of quick-drying, acrylic water-based paint, the easiest type of paint to work with. You can also buy a complete verdigris paint-effect kit. You will need a base coat, a coat of dark grey, and a coat each of turquoise and light green in toning shades to stipple over the base coat. Allow each coat to dry before applying the next, and make sure that all the paints are of the same type.

1 *Cover the outer sides of the bucket with a single coat of all-purpose primer and allow to dry.*

2 *Paint a dark grey coat of paint to cover the base coat, and allow it to dry thoroughly.*

3 *Using pale turquoise paint and a large stippling brush, dab colour unevenly over the dark grey base coat.*

stippling brush   Paint brush

Pale turquoise

Dark grey

Base coat

Pale green

4 *Using a pale green paint, dab the paint in areas where the previous coat is less apparent. Overlap in places to give a natural verdigris effect.*

5 *If you wish to make the verdigris effect more durable, apply a water-based matt acrylic varnish when the paint is completely dry.*

Leaf-covered Glass

A HOUSEHOLD TUMBLER CAN be turned into a smart container by covering it with a few glossy, tough, evergreen leaves, tied with green or natural raffia. You could also use a discarded tin in the same way, after washing it out well. A simple, single colour flower arrangement, like these small narcissus is ideal for this kind of container. Many different kinds of leaves can be used but they must be pliable – moistening helps to soften them. You can use large, leathery evergreen leaves, like those of *Magnolia grandiflora* as shown here, or ivy or laurel. Hosta leaves are another option: the creamy stripes of the variegated forms add a contrasting accent.

1 *Select some tough, large evergreen leaves and start to position the leaves around the glass, base down.*

2 *Add each new leaf, slightly overlapping its neighbour and ensuring that the leaf tips are level.*

3 *Wrap the raffia around the centre of the glass three or four times and tie the ends in a knot, then in a bow.*

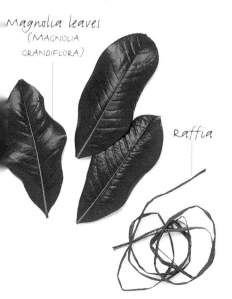

Magnolia leaves
(MAGNOLIA
GRANDIFLORA)

Raffia

4 *Trim off the bottoms of the leaves with sharp garden or kitchen scissors just fractionally below the base of the glass to create a neat finish.*

5 *Evergreen leaves retain their glossy sheen for a fairly long time so it is possible to use the covered container for several flower displays.*

Mossy Nest Basket

IF YOU HAVE no container of a suitable size or shape, you can make your own using chicken wire, a cut-down bin liner and some moss. It is a good choice for a small pot-grown plant, like this polyanthus, but would look just as good with a dome of dried roses, for example. Two polyanthus plants were used for this container. You will need a piece of chicken wire, 1in (2.5cm) gauge, double the height and width, plus a few inches, of the intended pot. Moss is readily available, either from a florist's or from the garden, when you scarify the lawn. This nest is quick to make and as the moss lasts well, it could also be used for a fresh flowers in a glass container.

1 *Cut the chicken wire into a suitably sized square and lay the moss over it. Carefully push up the sides of the wire to form the container.*

2 *Roll the chicken wire over at the rim of the container to seal the edges so that no sharp ends poke out. Push them well into the moss.*

3 *Start to mould the wire and moss to a suitable shape using your hands. Push and squeeze until it is the right size to take the pot or plant.*

Plastic liner

Moss

Chicken wire

4 *When the moss basket is correctly shaped, line with plastic and insert the plant into the well of the container.*

5 *The basket is easily remoulded to hold a different container. Poke in extra moss to hide any visible wire.*

Cloth Vase

A SIMPLE JAM JAR can be given a delightful disguise with a square of cotton cloth. You will need a rectangle of cloth big enough to cover the jar and allow you to wire the long ends of the rectangle into a twist of fabric. A collar of tissue paper around the base of the container disguises the jar further. Vary the fabric to suit the arrangement, but patterned material should be matched with single coloured flowers so that the overall effect is not conflicting. Simple colours and flowers, such as these red ranunculus with red and white gingham, work best as the look is unsophisticated. You also need some wire to secure the ties.

1 *Sit the jar in the centre of the cloth, and twist tissue paper to make a fat collar around the base of the jar.*

2 *Take up two long ends and pull them together to form a twisted tail of fabric at the neck of the jar.*

3 *Using strong florist's wire, pin the tail into place, wrapping the wire around the twist and securing it.*

Glass jar
Wire
Gingham fabric
Tissue paper

4 *Secure the opposite corners of cloth in the same way and adjust the fabric ties to conceal the wire.*

5 *This simple but smart container looks well on a kitchen window shelf or on a bedside table.*

Situations

for

FLOWERS

OST OF US find favourite places to display
flowers, from a small occasional table in the
hall or on a landing to the centre of a big
dining room table. This chapter takes a look at the many
possibilities for displaying flowers and offers inspirational
ideas on how to use different locations to best effect.

PERMANENT WINDOW DISPLAY

*A big window is the ideal place
for a striking arrangement of everlasting
parchment flowers.*

To CREATE A large, loose display suitable for a big window, you can opt for a range of flowers and flower forms – fresh, artificial or dried. For a sunny window, artificial flowers are ideal, as fresh flowers would soon wilt and the colour of dried flowers would rapidly fade.

Apart from considerations of longevity, the main point when designing a display for a large window is to ensure that it is sufficiently generous and echoes the overall form of the window itself. A large square bay needs an arrangement that is wider than it is tall, otherwise it will be dwarfed by the window space. Avoid pedestal arrangements in these settings – they will look strangely unbalanced.

▲ **ARTIFICIAL FLOWER ARRANGEMENT** ▶
In this traditional period setting, a Victorian glazed bowl filled with an exuberant display of larger-than-life parchment flowers and glycerine-dried foliage makes the perfect centrepiece on a desk in front of a large window.

CREATING *the Permanent* Window DISPLAY

For this arrangement, which was designed to sit in front of a large bay window,
you will need a large container, roughly 12in (30cm) tall and about the same in diameter.
We chose a ceramic bowl, but a wooden container would be just as suitable.

THIS ARRANGEMENT, designed to sit in front of a large bay window, has a rounded, domed shape, the structure created from foliage filled in with parchment flowers of various kinds.

For this display you will need a selection of artificial flowers (parchment flowers are ideal), and some sprigs of dried, small-leaved foliage. You can preserve foliage from your garden using glycerine (see page 123), or it can be bought from any good florist.

1 *Insert the blocks of oasis into the container, making sure that they are firmly wedged in the neck of the bowl. Cut them to fit if necessary. Then insert the framework of foliage, which will determine the height and width of the arrangement.*

Keep adding to the foliage to flesh out the framework, making sure some branches drop down below the level of the neck of the bowl to make a pleasing, almost circular shape.

INGREDIENTS
~
Parchment flowers of mixed types in toning colours

Stems of glycerined small-leaved foliage
~
2 blocks of dry oasis

2 *Fill the spaces in between the foliage with an assortment of parchment flowers in toning shades, ensuring they are well balanced across and through the arrangement.*

Hydrangea

Rosebud

Ornamental grass

Peony

Primula

Peony

Poppy

Cabbage rose

Iris

small rose

Oak (QUERCUS sp.)

Privet (LIGUSTRUM sp.)

Beech (FAGUS sp.)

Fresh Spring Flower Alternative

If you have a plentiful supply of your own garden flowers
and a large window that does not receive direct sunlight, fresh seasonal arrangements will
be just as successful as artificial displays in this setting.

WHETHER YOU USE garden or florist's flowers, aim to keep the arrangement loosely shaped and slightly soft-looking, using a wealth of foliage as well as flowers. The leaves will help fill in the gaps and give the arrangement substance, since no real flowers are as large or as space-filling as parchment flowers. Lilies and big hosta leaves, together with sprays of lady's mantle (*Alchemilla mollis*) make a good late spring alternative. In summer, a big

bowl of garden roses would be wonderful in this setting and in winter you could set a large bowl of forced bulbs (see pages 96-98) there instead, with arching canes over them to give height.

Flowering shrubs are also ideal for this kind of spreading arrangement – try the crab apple blossom shown below in spring and early summer, lilac or mock orange (*Philadelphus*) later in the summer and in winter twigs, hollies and colourful berries.

▼ **SPRING FRESHNESS**
Pinks and greens set the colour theme of this arrangement of spring blossom mixed with florist's gerberas. The bright pink of the gerberas is softened by the paler pink of the cherry blossom and the white of the crab apple blossom. Vivid green privet leaves provide the perfect tonal foil and the pink and white china bowl is an ideal container in terms of size, shape and colour to complement the freshness and generous proportions of the arrangement.

Privet
(LIGUSTRUM *sp.*)

Crab apple
blossom
(MALUS *sp.*)

Gerbera

Cherry blossom
(PRUNUS *sp.*)

Fresh Summer Flower Alternative

*In the summer months, there is a wealth of garden border flowers
to choose from, plus a good selection of florist's flowers. Whites, pinks, mauves,
greens and blues are the predominant colours.*

A SUMMER ARRANGEMENT should look light and fresh. If you incorporate a good selection of foliage to act as a foil to the flowers, it will give the display more body, while the flowers themselves will be highlighted against the darker background. Simple, naturally arranged displays that make the most of the abundance of plants available in this season are the most suitable and the most effective. Try to get a good mixture of textures to give the display greater interest and appeal.

A bucket or deep, fairly broad-necked vase is ideal for an arrangement that is as wide as it is tall. Choose a container that blends well with the flower forms and colours chosen. Garden roses look wonderful in silver tureens while more formal arrangements, like those below, look good in simple metal containers.

▼ ARCHITECTURAL SUMMER FLOWERS
This cool white and green display is created from lilies, florist's roses and star of Bethlehem, backed by eucalyptus foliage and viburnum foliage and flowers. The lilies and the eucalyptus provide the core structure, and the other flowers are then positioned between them to give a simple, rounded outline. The restrained colour scheme is set off by the neutral-toned container: a coloured vase would be distracting.

Eucalyptus

White florist's roses
(ROSA sp.)

Lily
(LILIUM
LONGIFLORUM)

star of
Bethlehem
(ORNITHOGALUM

Viburnum
(VIBURNUM TINUS)

Ivy
(HEDERA sp.)

Cotoneaster berries

Holly
(ILEX sp.)

Larch cones
(LARIX sp.)

Hazel
(CORYLUS sp.)

Amaryllis
(HIPPEASTRUM hybrid)

Ivy berries
(HEDERA sp.)

Fresh Winter Foliage Alternative

*In the winter months, make the most of twigs,
brightly coloured berries and evergreen foliage, perhaps with a few
florist's flowers to spice up the arrangement.*

AT THIS TIME of year, you will have to look a little harder for suitable material for flower arrangements, but combinations of wintry leaves and branches providing shape and texture, as well as any seed heads and berries still around, can prove surprisingly effective as a rich note of colour. If you have any winter-flowering shrubs in your garden, it is well worth finding a simple glass vase in which to create a spreading display of their branches – witch hazel (*Hamamelis mollis*) is a

good example, as are *Mahonia japonica* and the sloe berries (*Prunus spinosa*) shown on page 42.

Florists often have a selection of coloured dogwood stems and these go well with the Singapore orchids and amaryllis flowers that appear not long before Christmas. Arrangements with a red and green theme are particularly appropriate at this time of year, and holly leaves, especially the variegated gold and green forms, are an ideal foil for orange and red flowers and berries.

▲ RED, GOLD AND GREEN

This spreading arrangement, contained in a simple glass vase with a wide neck, has a strongly focused colour theme with scarlet as the main colour, provided principally by the big showy blooms of amaryllis, supported by cotoneaster berries. Larch cones and twigs, holly leaves and hazel twigs give texture to the display. Note how the longer stems of hazel, larch and cotoneaster have been used to break up the rounded outline of the arrangement and make it less dense.

WINDOW-SILL HERB BASKET

A sunny kitchen window-sill is the ideal situation for this collection of fresh culinary herbs.

KEEN COOKS LIKE to have a selection of fresh herbs to hand. These usually sit in their plastic pots in front of the kitchen window, but, with some thought, they can be turned into an attractive decoration in their own right, simply by making a suitable container to hide the less-than-beautiful pots in which they are purchased.

This moss basket is easily made from a cut-down washing powder carton, which is then wrapped with moss fixed in position with green garden string. It will last for two to three weeks and makes a suitable container for any simple collection of small pot plants.

▶ **INDOOR HERB GARDEN**
A couple of pots of parsley, and one of sage, sit in front of the kitchen window, grouped in the moss pot. A mixture of purple and green basil would also look good.

▲ **MATCHING UP CONTAINERS**
If you do not want to make a moss basket, group your herbs together in similarly coloured or styled containers. Here, small wooden and clay pots have been given a decorative paint finish to create a matching display.

CREATING *the*
Window-sill Herb BASKET

For this basket, you will need an empty washing powder carton, moss and
garden string or reel wire, in addition to the selection of herbs which make up the central theme of
the display. Choose herbs both for their flavour and their appearance.

THIS MOSS BASKET is very simple to make; you will need to find a suitable carton or box to take the pots of herbs you intend to put in it. An old washing powder box is the most successful. These are quite tough to cut, and you will probably have to use both a very sharp knife (such as a craft knife), plus stout kitchen scissors to trim it. Bind the moss to the carton with garden string, florists' reel wire or raffia if you prefer – use either natural or dark green. The choice of herbs depends on what is available and whichever herbs you use most often.

1 *Cut the base of the carton, having checked the height to ensure it disguises the pots – normally about 6in (15cm) is enough. Trim with scissors.*

2 *Start to bind the moss to the carton base. If you turn the carton on its side, you will find this easier. Use twine or reel wire to secure the moss.*

INGREDIENTS
~
Parsley (Petroselinum)
Sage (Salvia officinalis)
Moss
~
Soap powder carton
Craft knife and scissors
Garden string or reel wire
Bin liner

3 *Fasten the twine at the corner with a knot and cut the ends. You can bind the twine in more than one place if needed to fix the moss securely.*

4 *Line the inside of the carton with a cut down bin liner, to make a waterproof interior. You can then water the herbs when necessary.*

Parsley
(PETROSELINUM)

Sage (SALVIA OFFICINALIS)

Moss

Fresh Flower Alternative

*Unassuming displays of plants, in household objects, can have
a quiet charm of their own. You do not need lavish displays or handsome
containers – just a few well-chosen individual flowers.*

I F YOU HAVE a cool window (south-facing windows are generally too hot for fresh flowers in summer), you can use a table, ledge or shelf in front of it for a massed display of simple, small containers filled with equally simple flowers. Little displays like these add colour and life to rooms such as kitchens and bathrooms that tend not to be highly decorated.

You can use this situation to create a home for any flowers you happen to rescue from the garden – perhaps a few storm-blown flowers, an exquisite single bloom or the odd plant whose stem has broken – or a surplus stem from a more elaborate arrangement elsewhere in the house.

Tumblers, little florist's buckets, and even eggcups can be used to create an unimposing, but effective, display. It is best if the containers are similar in texture or style, and if the flowers are roughly similar in scale.

▼ GROUPED ARRANGEMENT
Instead of pots of herbs, you can group a collection of flowers from the garden in front of the kitchen window. Plain containers are best. Restrict the colour range for greatest impact. Here, white campanula, valerian, campion, cosmos and aquilegia flowers contrast with the deep red of astrantia and the purple of African violets and pansies, with the pale green of lady's mantle setting off and complementing both tonal ranges.

AUTUMN
TABLE CENTRE

*This handsome table centre is ideal for
a big dining-room table, the autumnal tones
of gold, russet and bronze predominating.*

Wʜᴇɴ ᴄʀᴇᴀᴛɪɴɢ arrangements for table
centres you need to take into account
not only aesthetic considerations, such as the
colours of the room's decoration and of any
china or table linen you may be using, but
practical considerations as well: the size and
shape of the table, for example. For an informal
lunch or dinner party at a table seating up to
ten, you also need to consider whether the
guests will be able to see over the top of the
arrangement. It is not conducive to conversa-
tion if you cannot see the person directly
opposite you at the table because a tall flower
arrangement is blocking the view.

It is always a good idea to use whatever
seasonal material is to hand in the garden,
either on its own or to supplement flowers
from a florist. Gather berries and fruit in
autumn and winter, spring bulbs early in the
year and perennials in summer.

◄ MELLOW FRUITFULNESS ▲

This long, low table centre arrangement, made on a tray or platter, is ideal for a large oval or rectangular table. The deep reds, golds and russets of the autumn fruit, foliage and vegetables complement this dining-room particularly well, harmonizing with the terracotta walls and the richly coloured mahogany table, and creating a warm glow in the centre.

CREATING *the Autumn* TABLE CENTRE

This table centre makes use of autumn harvest produce and hedgerow material. You can make it from whatever you can find locally, by combining a few large vegetables and fruits (artichokes, sweetcorn, gourds and pomegranates) with smaller fruiting and berrying shrubs.

USE A BLOCK of pre-soaked wet oasis to form the basic structure into which pyracantha berries, rose hips and artichoke heads are inserted. This provides the basic frame, then the rest of the ingredients are loosely piled around it. There are no formal instructions for making this kind of arrangement, except that you first need to create a base and then put a layer of larger fruits and vegetables at the bottom to make a rough platform onto which the other ingredients are piled. The overall shape should be a very rough pyramid, and it should look natural and slightly asymmetrical rather than appearing rigidly contrived.

You can make the arrangement in the kitchen, and carry it through to the table, to prevent the dining table becoming scratched or stained.

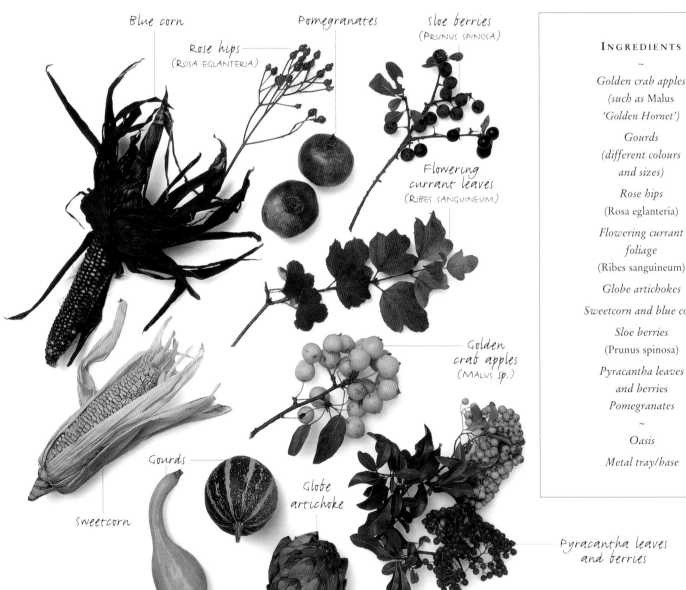

Blue corn

Rose hips
(ROSA EGLANTERIA)

Pomegranates

sloe berries
(PRUNUS SPINOSA)

Flowering
currant leaves
(RIBES SANGUINEUM)

Golden
crab apples
(MALUS sp.)

Gourds

Globe
artichoke

sweetcorn

Pyracantha leaves
and berries

INGREDIENTS

~

Golden crab apples
(such as Malus
'Golden Hornet')

Gourds
(different colours
and sizes)

Rose hips
(Rosa eglanteria)

Flowering currant
foliage
(Ribes sanguineum)

Globe artichokes

Sweetcorn and blue corn

Sloe berries
(Prunus spinosa)

Pyracantha leaves
and berries

Pomegranates

~

Oasis

Metal tray/base

1 Place a block of pre-soaked wet oasis on a large platter, about 18in (45cm) long and half as wide. Insert four sprigs of golden crab apples into each end of the block to form the basic structure, allowing the crab apples to spill over the sides of the tray.

2 Arrange the gourds around the block of oasis, and insert some of the rose hip sprigs into it to flesh out the structure. Lay the sprigs of flowering currant foliage in between the gourds and the rose hips. The artichoke heads can be pushed into the oasis to form the second tier.

3 Continue to add the artichoke heads to form the upper level, as well as the cobs of sweetcorn and blue corn, angled sideways. Allow the dried white leaves of the sweetcorn to show, as this provides a good colour contrast with the dark berries and fruits.

4 Add the sprigs of sloe and pyracantha berries to provide colour contrast, first removing most of their green leaves. Add the pomegranates in any gaps, to balance the shapes and colours, and continue to add foliage, hips and berries to fill in the overall shape.

Alternative Autumn Table Centre

This alternative autumn table centre, arranged on a raised glass cake stand, is suitable for a small table and is a decorative way to display fruit for dessert.

A ROUND TABLE could have a smaller fruit and flower centrepiece, arranged on a cake stand – in this case a glass one. Again, a block of oasis provides the central core, into which the hydrangea heads are inserted. Hydrangea dries exceptionally well (see page 123) and provides year-round decorative floral material.

▶ **FLOWERS AND FRUIT**
The russet hues of pomegranates, cherries and apples mingle with the soft, deep reddish-pink hydrangea florets. This simple fruit display makes an elegant centrepiece for an autumn dinner party.

Hydrangea leaves & flowers (HYDRANGEA MACROPHYLLA)

Cherry

Apple

Pomegranate

Autumn Fruit Alternative

This 'apple tree', created in a glass vase filled with apples, makes use of
windfall apples, and a few leaves from the apple tree. The tree is constructed using a stemmed
glass in the centre of the main glass container.

IT IS A GOOD IDEA to make table centre arrangements with the food you intend to serve at a dinner party, particularly with starters and desserts. This apple table centre, however, is intended to last slightly longer and can stay on the table for a few days. It makes a decorative display out of windfalls of apples, but pears could equally well be used. The proportions of the tree are an important element in its design. Pay particular attention to the style and form of container you use, as it plays a major role in the overall look of the arrangement. A rectangular, slightly squat glass container is ideal, both to show off the apples and to provide a solid trunk-like base for the 'tree'. A few red plastic cherries, plus fresh sprigs of leaves from the real tree, are all you need in addition to a good number of small apples.

CONSTRUCTION TIP *Insert a glass in the centre of the container and fill it with fresh water. You can then start to fill the outer container with apples and bright red plastic cherries (which look very realistic when mixed among the apples) to hide the inner glass and make the container a colourful element in the whole centrepiece.*

◄ MOCK APPLE TREE
This is a marvellous way to use up windfalls, as you can turn the apples round to disguise any blemishes. Very bruised fruit should be discarded (or the bruised parts cut out) as the fruit will go off too quickly otherwise. Polish each windfall apple with a soft cloth to give the fruit a good sheen. Twigs of apple foliage are inserted into the small glass, then each apple is skewered on to a wooden pea stick or plant support – in dark green to merge with the foliage – and inserted into the central glass, to look as though the apples are growing on the 'tree'.

Polished
windfall apples

Apple tree
twigs and
leaves

Red plastic
cherries

Summer Fruit Bowl

To give a fruit bowl more life and colour and to make it an attractive feature on the dining table, add a few sprigs of flowers to the collection of fruit. Use whatever is seasonally appropriate and if flowers are in short supply use leaves of shrubs or herbs.

GLASS BOWLS ARE ideal for displaying fruit, especially bowls with a small stem which raise the fruit up to view. A bowl filled with fruit and flowers, like this one, makes an excellent edible table centre display for a round table. It is best to choose flowers which complement the fruit in terms of colour and which are not too overwhelming or pick some large, soft leaves and intersperse them with fruit.

◄ SUMMER FRUIT BOWL
A colourful bowl of summer fruit – grapes, apples, pears and peaches in this case – is given a little extra decoration by adding a few clematis sprigs (clematis viticella) tucked in among the fruit. You can copy this simple theme with whatever fruit (or nuts) you put on the table. A few scented flowers, such as honeysuckle or jasmine, would make a delightful addition to a bowl of peaches, say, at a summer dinner.

Cheese and Fruit Basket

You can turn a simple cheese platter into an attractive centrepiece for a table by adding fruit and a few leaves to create an inviting display. Use whatever foliage is to hand in the garden, as long as it is not poisonous, of course.

FOR THE PLATTER, choose fruit and nuts that have a naturally attractive colour and shape – figs, red William pears, grapes and walnuts are ideal, setting off the cheese to perfection. A few leaves – apple leaves, purple-leaved sage and rose leaves – that echo the colours and tones of the fruit, help to soften the overall look.

► CHEESE AND FRUIT BASKET
You can make a decorative table centre out of the dessert by arranging cheese and fruit on a suitable container. The shallow, round, plaited straw platter used here is ideal. Line it with a crisply starched white napkin and display the cheese and fruit on it with a few sprigs of foliage to form a pleasing picture.

Dates

Figs

Pears

Cherry tomatoes

sage leaves
(SALVIA OFFICINALIS)

Grapes

LOW TABLE ARRANGEMENT

Of all the situations for flowers, low tables are the most accommodating. Use them for seasonal displays of small flowers in neat, dome-shaped arrangements.

ISPLAYS FOR LOW tables must not dwarf the table or look out of scale with its proportions. Fresh, dried and pot-grown plants are all suitable for this kind of setting, but keep in mind that the arrangement should be composed 'in the round'. In other words, it has to look good from all sides. This normally means that the centre of the arrangement is the highest point, and the sides slope down towards the edges of the container. Arrangements could be composed of a single flower type, blocked together in a dome shape – tightly packed florist's roses, perhaps, or

maybe two or three generous bunches of tulips, the stems considerably shortened to make a neatly rounded display.

Keep the colour palette of the arrangement in sympathy with the decoration scheme, either by picking up one of the colour accents or by creating a softly harmonizing colour scheme in shades of the hues used in the decoration of the room.

▼ **ALL-ROUND VIEW** ►
This low display employs large-headed chrysanthemum flowers cut down to size and integrated with interesting foliage. Texture is particularly important when an arrangement is seen from close quarters.

CREATING *the Low Table*
ARRANGEMENT

This low table display, designed to be seen from all sides, requires a
central block of oasis in which to construct the dome-shaped arrangement,
and a suitable round container.

THIS ATTRACTIVE LITTLE table arrangement has a traditional, formal basis in which the larger flowers are used, along with the foliage, to block out a neat symmetrical shape. Choose colours and textures that will balance each other and give a varied effect to the arrangement. Note how the striking leucadendron leaves create a strong framework for the heads of the chrysanthemums.

Using more adventurous colour combinations, or those that break the unwritten rules of colour harmonies, can give a display great impact. The old adage has it that 'blue and green should never be seen'. This arrangement certainly disproves it!

1 *Trim a block of pre-soaked florist's oasis to shape and fit it into the container required – in this case a small, circular glass dish, leaving 2in (5cm) above the rim of the container. Fill out any spaces with garden moss.*

2 *Trim the stalks of the chrysanthemum flowerheads down to the length required and begin by inserting them at intervals around the perimeter of the block to create a 'collar' for the arrangement.*

Viburnum berries
(VIBURNUM OPULUS)

Agapanthus
(AGAPANTHUS AFRICANUS)

LEUCADENDRON
'safari sunset'

Cape green
(ABROTAN)

Chrysanthemum
(CHRYSANTHEMUM 'shamrock')

INGREDIENTS

~

Chrysanthemum
(Chrysanthemum 'Shamrock')

Viburnum berries
(Viburnum opulus)

'Safari Sunset'
Leucadendron

Cape Green
(Abrotan)

Agapanthus
(Agapanthus africanus)

~

Florist's oasis

Garden moss

3 Insert small sprigs of the glossy-leaved Leucadendron 'Safari Sunset' between the chrysanthemum heads to provide contrast in texture and colour and to form a general overall structure.

4 Begin to flesh out the arrangement by filling spaces with cape green berries and inserting the delicate blue heads of the agapanthus flowers. Cut down the agapanthus stems to around 6in (15cm) in length first.

5 Finally, insert clusters of red viburnum berries to add warmth to the colour range and provide bulk to the arrangement. Remember to keep turning the container so that the arrangement is balanced from all sides.

Small Low Table Alternative

For a small side table, this little mossy basket filled with pansies in toning colours is pretty and long-lasting.

IN ADDITION TO constructing fresh flower arrangements for low tables, you can make a simple but effective display using a few pots of striking flowers, like the winter pansies shown here in toning shades of mauve and deep purple. Transferring the pot-grown plants into attractive small terracotta pots, and filling any space in the container with moss is all that is required to create an eye-catching and long-lasting display. Flowering plant displays are best in a sunny position. Once the pansies are past their best, you can plant them in the garden. Keep the pots well watered and if the container is not waterproof use a plastic liner (see page 119). The compost should be kept moist but not waterlogged.

▶ INDOOR FLOWER BED
Replanting the winter pansies in earthy terracotta pots gives this low table display a country style, especially when combined with garden moss and the wicker container.

HALL AND LANDING ARRANGEMENTS

For hallways and landings, tall, narrow arrangements are often the most successful, providing a welcoming atmosphere without obstruction. Ideally these arrangements should have a clear outline and interesting textural quality.

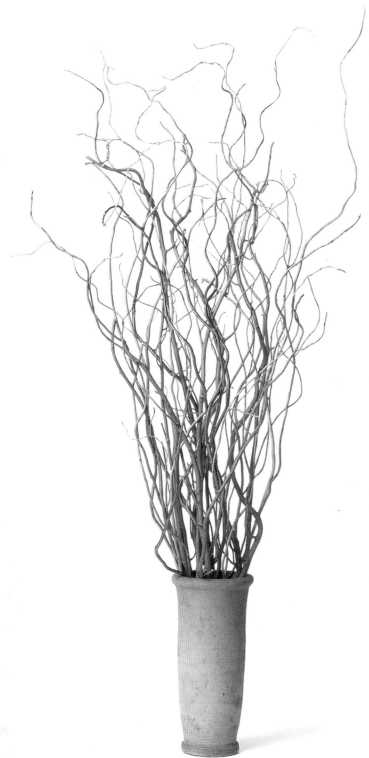

HALLS AND LANDINGS, being often narrow and fairly dark, are notoriously difficult to decorate. Because they tend to have a large expanse of wall area, any floral arrangement needs to be striking and fairly large without impinging too much on the traffic that passes through these linking spaces in the house. A small side table or a narrow window shelf are the ideal locations for an arrangement. If your landing is large enough, you can put a small table against the banisters themselves, as shown here.

Tall narrow arrangements are usually the most successful, and the form should be strong and clear in outline. This predominantly yellow and green arrangement is an autumnal fresh flower arrangement; a simple long-lasting winter alternative would be twisted hazel or willow twigs in a tall vase (see left). In spring, a bowl of tall scented narcissi (see page 96) or twigs of forsythia would work well in this situation, and in summer an armful of lilac. Silk or dried flowers are always a good choice in these positions, particularly when the daylight levels are very low.

◄ **PERMANENT HALLWAY DISPLAY**
A tall, elegant vase filled with twisted willow (Salix matsudana 'Tortuosa') or twisted hazel (Corylus avellana 'Contorta') would make a good permanent feature in a very narrow hallway.

▶▶ **AUTUMN LANDING ARRANGEMENT**
This display has a tall, strong triangular structure and a bold impact. Rich in autumnal colours, it combines a dramatic shape with strongly contrasted light and dark tones.

CREATING *the Autumn* Landing ARRANGEMENT

This striking arrangement of large flowers and architectural foliage is
best seen against a simple background that does not detract from its dramatic qualities.
A plain container is ideal for this kind of display.

THIS SUNFLOWER arrangement gains its strength and simplicity from using large, handsome flowers and clearly defined foliage forms. When making this kind of display, make sure that it is neither too tall nor too wide for the container. A triangular shape, whereby the width at the base of the arrangement is roughly equal to the length of each side of the triangle, and the height of the container equal to half the base of the triangle, works best. Don't choose too narrow a container or the arrangement will look mean.

CONSTRUCTION TIP *Remove all the petals from a few of the sunflowers. The remaining dark centres with their spiky leaves add depth and form.*

1 *Create a collar round the top of the container by adding the ivy and amaranthus to spill over the edge. Insert the feathery golden rod at the back to build up the outline and then add the hypericum berries.*

Bulrush
(TYPHA LATIFOLIA)

Sunflower
(HELIANTHUS)

Golden rod
(SOLIDAGO)

Hypericum

Alstroemeria

Variegated ivy
(HEDERA HELIX)

Amaranthus

INGREDIENTS
~

Bulrushes (Typha latifolia)

Golden rod (Solidago)

Variegated ivy (Hedera helix)

Sunflowers (Helianthus)

Alstroemeria

Hypericum

Amaranthus

2 *Add the yellow alstroemeria and then the sunflowers to provide a bright focal point. Add the bulrushes for extra height.*

Landing Window Alternative

*A small table in front of a landing (or hall) window
can provide a permanent situation for fresh or artificial flowers. The backlighting from
the window enhances the form of the flowers.*

A SMALL TABLE in front of a cool window (ideally with north or east facing light) is an ideal place to display flowers that have a beautiful shape and form, like the parrot tulips below. Tulips are more graceful when they are relaxed and slightly drooping (although they do need conditioning first; see page 117). If the window is sunny, opt for silk flowers instead.

▶ **SILK TULIPS**
When fresh tulips are not available, silk ones, mixed with real foliage, make a colourful alternative.

▼ **PARROT TULIPS**
At this narrow north-facing landing window, with its rather cool light, rich pink parrot tulips arranged informally in a jug create a feeling of glowing warmth.

Simple Hall Arrangements

Occasional tables offer great scope for changing displays of flowers through the seasons. Very simple displays, with a strong colour theme, are ideal for these situations.

MANY PEOPLE HAVE a favourite place for flowers, perhaps a small hall table or an occasional table in the living room. If you position a mirror behind the table, you will increase the effect of any display enormously. If you do this, you need to make sure that the display is worked 'in the round' – in other words, it looks good from all sides rather than being the flat 'fan shape' that is usually used for narrow tables set against a wall.

▶ **INFORMAL GROUPED DISPLAY**
This pine table has been filled with a display of yellow florist's and garden flowers – tulips, forsythia and golden rod – in terracotta pots of varying sizes.

▼ **INFORMAL SINGLE DISPLAY**
A simple arrangement of hyacinths and tulips in a blue and white china jug and bowl looks pretty on a small washstand in a country-style setting.

EUCALYPTUS POTS IN A CUPBOARD

Cupboards and shelves can be used to show off small displays of flowers. Dried and parchment flowers are ideal for darker places; fresh flowers and pot plants for better-lit areas.

◀ CUPBOARD DISPLAY ▶

The shelves of this carved Swedish-style cupboard provide a frame for terracotta pots. The pots are simply painted to suit the pastel shades and natural wood of their setting and are filled with dried eucalyptus and red silk roses. The symmetrical positioning of the pots on the shelves has helped to create a formal pattern that enhances the decorative detailing of the cupboard. Arrangements that rely on repetition to create a design should be kept simple so that the eye is not distracted by one element but takes in the picture as a whole.

SMALL ARRANGEMENTS come into their own when positioned on shelves or in cupboards. What the arrangements lack in size, they make up for in the impact of repeating colours and shapes. Small terracotta containers can be filled with either dried or pot-grown plants, depending on the light available; baskets can be filled with aromatic dried herbs or flowers. Make sure that the style, texture and form of the pots and arrangements are in keeping with the surroundings. Small baskets of country flowers suit a pine kitchen; more formal pots look better on plain glass shelves.

The colours you use will depend on the setting: traditional in style or bright and contemporary. Within this framework, you can choose flowers to contrast with an existing colour scheme or you can provide a further colour accent, picking up a predominant colour from fabrics or wallpaper.

CREATING *the* Eucalyptus POTS

*Eucalyptus is a favourite foliage plant for adding depth and variety to cut flowers because
of its long-lasting grey-green colour and the interesting shape of its young leaves. The leaves dry well and
here provide a subdued, textured background for the deep red of the silk roses.*

THE SOFT PINKISH beige of the terracotta pots is a perfect foil for dyed and glycerine-dried eucalyptus, and red silk roses add a colour accent.

Any neat foliage, dried or fresh, can be used for this pot. Box or bay work equally well, and you can vary the colour of the accent flowers according to the colour of the pot you use. A bright yellow glazed pot, for example, would benefit from a few gold chrysanthemum heads added to the foliage.

INGREDIENTS

~

Dyed and glycerine-dried eucalyptus

Silk roses

~

Dry oasis

Florist's wire

Dyed and glycerine-dried
eucalyptus

silk rose

1 *Snip the eucalyptus leaves into several short lengths. For a pot that is 6in (15cm) tall, cut sprigs about 6in (15cm) long. Cut a length of florist's wire and use this to wind a few sprigs of foliage together, leaving enough wire to form a stem.*

2 *Snip off any surplus leaves from the small bunches of leaves so that they will form a smooth shape. Insert the eucalyptus sprigs into the block of oasis. Begin in the centre where the arrangement will be at its highest point and then work around it.*

3 *Once you have created a satisfactory, smooth round shape with the foliage, you can insert the silk flowers into the oasis. Space them around the arrangement in any gaps you find between the leaves, until you have achieved a balanced effect.*

CONSTRUCTION TIP *Once the foliage has all been inserted into the oasis, and before the roses are added, trim off any whiskery stalks with a sharp pair of scissors to ensure that the arrangement has an attractively rounded 'ball' shape.*

Cupboard-top Display

Cupboard tops are an ideal place to display collections of dried flowers, either tied loosely
in bunches or gathered in baskets. Select a single colour theme such as yellow – sunflowers and achillea,
for example – or, against a plain background, randomly mix shades of blue and pink.

FLOWERS ON TOP of a cupboard add a decorative country appeal. Dried flowers are the best choice since they last well, and do not need replacing too frequently. For kitchens and dining rooms a simple, natural arrangement works best and if you have a garden you can dry flowers from your borders to enhance your shelves and cupboards in this way (see page 120).

In the arrangement below, the dried flowers form part of a combined display with rustic earthenware and baskets. You can equally well use baskets to display the flowers, particularly if you tilt the baskets on their sides so that the contents appear to be spilling out naturally along the shelf.

Among the best flowers for such arrangements, all easily dried on a kitchen rack, are allium and poppy heads, hydrangea florets, helichrysum and roses, and herbs such as marjoram, lavender and thyme.

▼ **A RUSTIC DISPLAY**
The gold tones of the wall and the jug create a feeling of warmth, coupled with the gold, pink and red flowers. Dried flowers have subtle, gentle colours that work well with the natural tones of wood and wicker. The spiky heads of allium and the fresh gold of achillea flowers on the left merge into the smoky pinky-blue of the hydrangea florets, the dried pink roses and the darker foliage of marjoram. Grasses and poppy seedheads add textural variety.

Shelf Display with Fresh Flowers

Two or three repeating posies of flowers brighten up and focus attention
on shelves displaying china. Here, a spring combination of miniature narcissus and euphorbia has been
simply arranged in kitchen glasses in front of a collection of earthenware.

SHELVES DISPLAYING CHINA will often have space for miniature arrangements. These are most effective when you use colours that harmonize or contrast with the china and repeat the display so that a frieze-like effect is achieved. A collection of blue china would be enhanced by a few pots of blue pansies, while oatmeal glazed earthenware makes a backdrop for the yellow and green display of miniature daffodils (*Narcissus* 'Tête à Tête') and euphorbia shown here. Keep the containers plain to focus on the flowers and china. Dried flowers also look good in this setting: for example, you could put clay pots of lavender on a pine dresser with blue and white china.

▼ **SPRING POSIES**
These three simple posies of narcissus look particularly pretty against the oatmeal earthenware. Simple country china makes a perfect background for this kind of natural-looking display, and the impact is gained from the repeating nature of the arrangement: one small posy on its own would look insignificant.

Miniature Flower Theatre

Shelves in glass-fronted cupboards or in small
alcoves are the ideal place to create a tiny flower theatre, using
repeating pots of the same flowers.

I N THIS SMALL cupboard, its shelf
edgings prettily decorated with a
narrow lace border, small terracotta
pots have been filled with matching
displays of pot-grown *Bellis perennis*, an
attractive pink-flowered daisy.

You can create many different vari-
ations on this theme, using either fresh
flowers, dried flowers or pot-grown
plants. Plants should be placed out in
the garden after a week or so, as they
will need light to thrive after ten days
or so. If you wish, you can have a permanent display area, like this one, and
change the contents every couple of
weeks or so, rather like a play changes
in a repertory theatre. You can adapt
the flowers to suit the season – spring
pastels, autumn golds and winter
berries. Dried or silk flowers can stay in
position for as long as you wish.

Make sure that the pots, and the
contents, are in proportion to the space
around them so that they make an
attractive display in keeping with their
setting. You could vary the number of
pots on the shelves and use different
sizes on different shelves if the latter
are not evenly spaced.

► FLOWER TIERS
Bellis perennis plants are an ideal shape
and size for these small terracotta pots, as
their height is roughly the same as the pot
itself, neatly filling most of the space between
the shelves. Alternative flower choices
might be small geraniums (Pelargonium) or
verbena. In a more modern setting, pots of
little ferns would look good and would
cope for longer with a shady position.

ARTIFICIAL FLOWER FIREPLACE DISPLAY

*Fireplaces are ideal spaces for large
displays of dried or artificial flowers which help to
fill the fireplace recess.*

I N SUMMER, WHEN supplies are plentiful and inexpensive, fresh flowers can be used as fireplace arrangements, but in autumn and spring, on days when you do not need a fire in the hearth, you can use a dried or silk flower arrangement to fill the gap.

Fresh or dried, the flowers need to be bold and dramatic enough to fill the space and catch the eye. Choose colours that blend well with the surrounding decor and flesh out the arrangement with foliage which ideally should be long enough to break the shape of the fireplace. The final shape of the arrangement will depend on the form of the fireplace, but most will need to be roughly square or oval.

▼ FIREPLACE DISPLAY ▶

A handsome marble fireplace is filled with a rich selection of large-headed dried and parchment flowers in autumnal shades of gold, russet and green. The flowers were arranged in situ *to ensure that the size and shape of the arrangement fill the space attractively.*

CREATING *the Artificial Flower*
FIREPLACE DISPLAY

Generous amounts of flowers are needed for a large display.
Although dried and artificial flowers are expensive, do not skimp on the quantities –
as the flowers are everlasting, they are a good investment.

INGREDIENTS

~

Dyed, glycerine-dried eucalyptus

Dried Hydrangea arborescens *'Annabelle'*

Silk yarrow

Dried poppy seedheads
(Papaver)

Parchment peony

Silk freesia

Parchment rose

~

Oasis

YOU CAN USE all manner of dried or artificial flowers for a large, permanent display. The space is usually best filled with architectural-looking flowers with handsome flowerheads or striking foliage – hydrangea heads are ideal and dry very easily, if you have a bush or two in your garden; so are big striking tightly packed heads of yarrow (*Achillea millefolium*). Alternatively, a large stook of corn or barley can be stood in the grate, making a handsome focal point in a modern fireplace.

You will need a large container, such as a leather bucket or terracotta pot which is slightly wider at the rim than the base. The one used here was approximately 10in (25cm) tall and 12in (30cm) in diameter. Blocks of dry oasis should be inserted into the bucket, leaving 2in (5cm) protruding above the rim so that you can insert some flower stems into the sides of the oasis to create the width of the display.

Begin by creating the basic bones of the display using the tallest stems of foliage. Then insert the flowers between and around the stems, blocking in the shape by using the bigger flowerheads first. The poppy seedheads are best bunched into small groups to create greater impact.

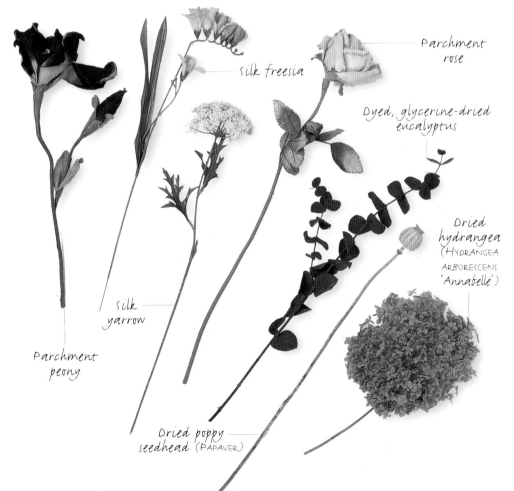

Parchment
rose

silk freesia

Dyed, glycerine-dried
eucalyptus

Dried
hydrangea
(HYDRANGEA
ARBORESCENS
'Annabelle')

silk
yarrow

Parchment
peony

Dried poppy
seedhead (PAPAVER)

1 *Having inserted the oasis into the bucket with roughly 2in (5cm) protruding above the rim of the container, insert the eucalyptus stems in a neat fan shape to fill the space in the fireplace.*

2 *Insert the hydrangea flowerheads, two low down and two nearer the top. Add poppy heads in small groups, and pale achillea in the gaps between.*

3 *Continue to flesh out the arrangement with roses, freesias and yellow achillea, balancing the colours and shapes throughout the display.*

4 *Check for any holes or gaps and fill with single flowers. Check the arrangement from both sides as well as from the front.*

Silk Flower Fireplace Alternative

If you prefer a more modern, less elaborate decor, then this simple jug of silk sunflowers is an ideal choice, backed up with a couple of potted plants to fill the hearth.

Arrangements do not need to be complicated to be eyecatching. Simple shapes and strong colours are the key to success, especially when the shapes, as here, make a strong statement in their own right. A similar style of arrangement could be created with fresh sunflowers or with hydrangea flowerheads. Make sure the container is equally simple and strong in form – a plain terracotta or ceramic jug is the ideal choice. Try to choose colours that complement the room's decor – here, yellow sunflowers pick up the bright yellow of the walls, creating a cheerful and relaxed atmosphere.

SUNFLOWERS AND FERNS
simple jug of silk sunflowers, flanked by two ferns – Nephrolepis exaltata *'Bostoniensis' and* Asplenium scolopendrium *'Marginatum' – makes an attractive feathery display in a modern fireplace.*

EUCALYPTUS WALL WREATH

Wreaths can be made from dried or fresh flowers, herbs or foliage – in circles or ovals – the material wired tightly to a supporting base.

WREATHS AND GARLANDS on doors give a welcoming feel and a swag or wreath can lift a bare expanse of wall. Whether gaily colourful or elegantly single-toned, they can provide a natural focal point. These hanging decorations need not be confined to seasonal festivities but can be used all year round, whether made with dried flowers, foliage or grasses to last for a while, or made from fresh material for a special occasion or seasonal uplift. Wreaths do not have to be elaborate. Relatively simple ones, made from just one flower or leaf form, can look particularly effective – a fine circlet or two of lavender, for instance, would look pretty on a bedroom wall. Pairs of wreaths or swags look good when positioned either side of a feature such as a large mirror or at each side of a chimney breast.

▲ EUCALYPTUS WREATH ▶

Hung on this sloping chimney breast, the small eucalyptus wreath creates a focus of interest on a difficult-to-decorate architectural feature. Wreaths are versatile and adaptable – they can be hung on chimney breasts, doors and cupboards or in windows. They come in a range of forms and colours, as the versions overleaf show.

CREATING *the* Eucalyptus Wall WREATH

*Some of the most successful wreaths are simple circles made of
just one kind of flower or leaf, like this eucalyptus wreath – the textural quality
of the material used becomes its chief asset.*

THIS SIMPLE WREATH makes a permanent adornment to a wall, and looks particularly good against plain walls in pale colours, or hanging in a window. You can also make a more decorative version by adding a few silk or dried flowers in a contrasting colour, in a similar way to the eucalyptus pots on page 56. Attach a wire stalk to the ends of the flowers and push them into the wreath at intervals.

INGREDIENTS

~

Dyed, glycerine dried eucalyptus

~

Heavy-duty florist's or gardening wire

Fine florist's wire

1 *To make the base for the eucalyptus wreath, form the heavy-gauge wire into a circle measuring about 10in (25cm) in diameter. Fasten the ends of the wire together by binding them securely with fine wire.*

2 *Cover the base of the ring with stems of eucalyptus, securing them by wrapping loosely with fine florist's wire. If the woody stems are too tough to bend, they can be snapped. Overlap the stems so that the ends do not show.*

Fine florist's wire

Dyed, glycerine-dried eucalyptus

Gardening wire

3 *Snip off some short sprigs of eucalyptus and group them into small bunches of three or four stems. Bind the sprigs by winding fine wire around them, then bind the bunches on to the wreath, overlapping the base of one bunch with the top of the next. Make a small wire loop to enable you to hang the wreath.*

Alternative Dried Flower Wreaths

Using just a single plant for a wreath focuses attention on the form of the wreath
which then becomes a design feature in its own right. Soft colours, like the pale yellows and muted
mauves of these two wreaths, blend well with most colour schemes.

THE TWO WREATHS here show how the form can vary. The flax seed wreath below is created on a wide moss-covered frame (see page 71), the little oval marjoram wreath (right) on a simple wire base (see opposite). When making small wreaths, choose the form of the wreath and the material you use according to the setting. Looser, softer plant materials such as wheat and grasses suit informal, cottage-style settings; more tightly packed, elegant, architectural forms would look good in a more modern setting.

▼ MARJORAM AND EUCALYPTUS WREATH
Dried marjoram flowers are highly scented. Tightly packed together and interspersed with eucalyptus leaves on an oval base, they make a pretty addition to an informal cottage setting. A ceramic jug filled with Leptospermum twigs tones with the wreath.

◄ FLAX SEED WREATH
The knobbly, papery texture of the small flax seeds contrast with the neat circle of this small wreath, making it suitable for both informal and formal settings.

FRESH HERB DOOR WREATH

This door wreath is not only very pretty, it is also deliciously scented.
It is made with fresh herbs and flowers, which will then dry successfully in situ. *The*
scent of the herbs as they are drying will fill the room for months.

FRESH HERBS MAKE wonderful components for a wreath. Choose whatever herbs you have in the garden, or can obtain, that are both colourful and scented. The major scented ingredients here are sage and lavender. Arrange bunches of herbs around the wreath in groups of four. Use the foliage for the base; the flowers can act as fillers between the foliage.

▼ **SCENTED WREATH**
This wreath is made up of purple and blue flowering herbs, such as lavender and borage, and coloured herb foliage, such as purple sage, with the lime green flowers of lady's mantle for contrast.

CREATING *the Fresh Herb* DOOR WREATH

To make the herb wreath you will need a wreath base which is a circle of wire about 10in (25cm) in diameter. The base is covered in garden moss to form the supporting structure for the flowers and foliage.

THE BASE OF the wreath is constructed first, by binding moss to the wire support with twine. Make sure the base is well padded with moss, and that this is securely fixed to it. You can use whatever herbs and other flowering plants you have to hand, but make sure that you have enough to create repeating bunches around the circle, since the impact is gained from the repeating groups of flower and foliage colour and form. Choose herbs with a strong toning colour theme to make the most impact.

1 *Position the moss on the base and take twine over and round both until the whole wreath base is covered.*

2 *Once all the moss is in place, and firmly fixed to the structure, tie the twine and snip it off at one side.*

3 *Using florist's wire, wrap about six sprigs of each herb into bunches, leaving a 4in (10cm) tail of wire.*

4 *Add the foliage herbs, four bunches at intervals around the wreath, with the stems facing inward.*

5 *Add the flowering plants, wiring four bunches at intervals, varying the angles at which they are laid.*

INGREDIENTS

~

Sage (Salvia officinalis), *Pearl everlasting* (Anaphalis), *Lavender* (Lavandula *sp.*), *Borage* (Borago), *Love-in-a-mist* (Nigella damascena), *Lady's mantle* (Alchemilla mollis), *Sea holly* (Eryngium), *Clary sage* (Salvia sclarea *var.* Turkestanica)

~

Wreath base, Moss, Twine Fine florist's wire

Sage (SALVIA OFFICINALIS 'PURPURASCENS')

Clary sage (SALVIA SCLAREA var. TURKESTANICA)

sea holly (ERYNGIUM)

Lady's mantle (ALCHEMILLA MOLLIS)

Pearl everlasting (ANAPHALIS)

Lavender (LAVANDULA sp.)

Love-in-a-mist (NIGELLA DAMASCENA)

Borage (BORAGO)

Displays for SPECIAL EVENTS

T HERE ARE OCCASIONS when you wish to create a truly striking display to celebrate a special event, from family parties to intimate dinners. This chapter offers a range of styles, using easily obtainable, inexpensive ingredients.

AL FRESCO
TABLE RUNNER

*Eating out of doors in summer
is one of the true pleasures of life. Decorate the
table simply but elegantly.*

THIS SUMMER LUNCH party
setting follows the best French
tradition of family and friends eating together under the shade of a
tree on long trestle tables, covered
with a crisp white cloth. Decorating
the table along the centre is the
perfect solution for a long narrow
table. This kind of arrangement is
very versatile – you can go for
either informality or elegance,
depending on how the rest of the
table is dressed. The flowers – two
kinds of rose and lady's mantle – are
simple and country-style in mood,
ideally suited to a relaxed family
gathering. They are elegant enough,
however, to grace a simple summer
wedding breakfast as well, in which
case make a buttonhole for each of
the guests from a rose and a couple
of sprigs of lady's mantle, and put it
on each plate.

◄ SUMMER GARLAND ▼

This table runner of flowers is simply constructed on a series of plastic trays filled with oasis, which are then disguised with foliage. Garden flowers provide the floral centre, but you could equally use simple florist's flowers if you have none of your own.

CREATING *the Al Fresco* TABLE RUNNER

*You will need a sufficient number of plastic oasis trays to run the length of
the table together with enough wet oasis to provide a base in each tray for the flowers.
Simple foliage and flowers are used for the arrangement.*

THOUGH THIS TABLE centre looks elaborate, it is actually fairly quick and easy to decorate once you have the ingredients prepared. Cut a block of oasis into slices 1in (2.5cm) deep and soak them for half an hour. Fill the trays with the strips of oasis. Collect the foliage and flowers together and group them on a large work surface.

INGREDIENTS
~

Freshly cut garden roses:
Rosa 'Sanders' White Rambler',
Rosa 'Iceberg'
Lady's mantle (Alchemilla mollis)
Foliage of varying types:
wisteria (Wisteria *sp.) and geranium*
(Pelargonium) *leaves*
~
*Four blocks of wet oasis
cut in half lengthways
Four plastic trays*

1 *Place each block of wet oasis, cut in half, in its tray and insert foliage around the rim to disguise the tray.*

2 *Use a few different leaves to add variety, and insert two or three into the top of the oasis to hide it.*

3 *Fill the spaces with sprigs of lady's mantle to fill the display and make a base for the roses.*

4 *Add the main flowers (in this case two different kinds of white rose), and scatter them in random fashion.*

ROSA
'sanders' white rambler'

ROSA
'iceberg'

Lady's mantle
(ALCHEMILLA
MOLLIS)

wisteria
leaves
(WISTERIA sp.)

Geranium leaf
(PELARGONIUM sp.)

CONSTRUCTION TIP *You can make up each tray complete, as here, and then join up the trays, or you can work* *each step on all the trays, adding first the foliage to all of them, then the lady's mantle, and finally the roses.*

Alternative Lunch Party Setting

Bright and cheerful, this table setting is simplicity itself.
Each place setting has its own arrangement of flowers in a tumbler,
colour - coordinated with the china and table linen.

I F YOU DO NOT want to make an elaborate table setting, or there simply is not enough room, a repeating display of individual small arrangements, either one to each place setting or perhaps in a row of three or four down the table centre, is a very easy way to decorate the table.

The main principle is to match the colour and form of the containers for the flowers, and the flowers themselves, to the colour scheme and style, of your china and table linen. The funky lime and green and orange scheme in this display was dictated by the colours of the cloth, chairs and containers. If you want to create a similarly modern-looking display but lack appropriate containers, you could paint recycled tins in bright primary colours – electric blue, pillar-box red or sunflower yellow. Fill each container with flowers in a different colour – such as red gazanias in the yellow tin, blue cornflowers in the red tin and yellow daisies in the blue tin.

▼ **ALTERNATIVE ARRANGEMENT**
If you do your best to match your flowers to the setting, you will always succeed in creating a brilliantly effective party piece. Here plain glass tumblers arranged in a row down the centre of the table and filled with simple summer flowers, such as gerbera, lady's mantle (Alchemilla mollis), safflower (Carthamus) and golden rod (Solidago) in golds, greens and oranges, echo the colours of the china, chairs and table linen to create a chic, coordinated but summery display in a garden room.

CANDLELIT SUPPER TABLE

Sometimes a special occasion deserves a beautiful setting. This small candle table centre adds a touch of romance and is ideal for an intimate dîner à deux.

CANDLELIGHT IS RENOWNED for its flattering qualities, and what could be nicer than to create a table centre around a candle for a special occasion supper or dinner? This particular supper was set out of doors in summer, but you could vary the ingredients depending on the season and according to what is available in the garden or in the shops at the time of year.

As with all candle and flower arrangements, never leave a lit candle unattended. If the candle starts to burn down, simply replace it but a thick white candle should normally last as long as the dinner will before it burns the arrangement as well!

Garden flowers are ideal for a simple al fresco table setting. Use those with soft, feathery blooms, like lady's mantle, or simple delicate forms (pansies or small clematis flowers) together with garden roses which have rather more substance and form (as well as a delightful scent). A simple leafy container, tied with raffia, matches the natural form of the arrangement.

▼ CREATING THE SETTING
A crisp white cloth adds a touch of elegance to a simple table setting and disguises the imperfections of outdoor furniture. The table setting needs to be in proportion with the shape and size of the table. The one shown here is ideal for a small table set for two.

▲ CANDLELIT CHARM

Candlelight is the most flattering and romantic lighting, but you will need a sheltered
setting. Small additional lights, created from tumblers filled with moss, throw extra light on
the table. Garden flares can also be used or a couple of lanterns hung from a wall or pergola.

CREATING *the Candlelit* *Supper* TABLE

The container for this arrangement is a glass tumbler,
filled with oasis to anchor the candle firmly, and partially
disguised with foliage tied in place with raffia.

ALTHOUGH THIS arrangement has several stages, it is not difficult to make. Tying the leaves onto the glass is fiddly and you will find it much easier if there is someone around to tie the raffia in place once you have positioned the leaves, although it can be done single-handed. The best candles to use are fat white church candles, because they burn down slowly. Use any large garden leaves to decorate the tumbler – hosta leaves were used in this instance but magnolia leaves also work well. Garden roses (*Rosa*), geraniums (*Pelargonium*), small pansies (*Viola* sp.), and lady's mantle (*Alchemilla mollis*) were used for the arrangement; these can be varied depending on what is available. Try to pick one dominant flower, and a couple of 'chorus'-style flowers to fill in the gaps.

1 *Fill the tumbler with wet oasis, which should stand proud of the container. Wedge it securely into the container.*

2 *Trim the oasis to within 1in (2.5cm) of the rim of the container, using a sharp kitchen knife or craft knife.*

3 *Wrap the leaves around the jar and tie with raffia. The base of the leaves overlap the base of the jar by 1in (2.5cm).*

Florist's spray rose (ROSA)

Pansy (VIOLA sp.)

Lady's mantle (ALCHEMILLA MOLLIS)

Hosta leaf (HOSTA sp.)

Geranium (PELARGONIUM sp.)

INGREDIENTS
~
Roses (Rosa)
Geraniums (Pelargonium *sp.*)
Lady's mantle (Alchemilla mollis)
Pansies (Viola *sp.*)
Hosta leaves (Hosta *sp.*)
~
Wet oasis
Candle
Heavy-duty wire
Florist's tape
Raffia

4 *Trim the base of the leaves level with the base of the jar, to create a neat, even base for the display.*

5 *Bind two or three prongs of heavy-duty wire to the base of the candle with florist's tape (or similar sticky tape).*

6 *Push the candle well down into the oasis to ensure it is secure. Fold back the tips of the leaves to make a star shape.*

7 *Start to insert the sprigs of lady's mantle evenly spaced into the oasis, encircling the candle.*

8 *Add the red roses (complete with leaves) and red geranium in the gaps between the lady's mantle.*

9 *Finally add a few delicate violas to the top of the display, spacing them around the candle, to finish off the arrangement.*

Single Candle Displays

A night light floating in a shallow glass bowl of water is the starting point for a glamorous dinner party place setting.

FOR A SUPPER party, you could make individual floating candle displays, with matching napkin decorations.

For this arrangement, purple heuchera (*Heuchera micrantha* 'Palace Purple') leaves are laid face down on the table around the base of a glass bowl, with leaves of lady's mantle (*Alchemilla mollis*) on top. Floating on the water in the bowl are the exotic flower heads of *Clematis* 'Mme Julia Correvon', interspersed with delicate sprays of bright green maidenhair fern (*Adiantum* sp.).

The napkins are embellished with a heuchera leaf and a fern frond.

▲ **SETTING A STYLE**
Rolled white damask napkins are given an extra degree of elegance by decorative foliage loosely bound on with green wire.

FESTIVE WINTER TABLE SETTING

Evergreen foliage, berries and cones, together with candles, create a strongly architectural arrangement for a dinner party table centre display.

T HIS ELEGANT TABLE setting is ideal for a winter dinner party: it uses only foliage, fir cones and seedheads that can be collected from a winter garden. It is easy to make but shows how effective just two colours – green and white – can be and how, by keeping the colour range simple, it blends in well with most colour schemes and styles of furniture – whether a sophisticated town setting or a simple country-style interior.

Winter foliage has its own special qualities. In this arrangement the glossy fatsia leaves reflect the soft candlelight, the variegated holly adds a central touch of brightness and the fir cones contribute texture and height. If you want to adapt the setting for a festive occasion, replace the white candles with red ones for Christmas and choose scarlet berries instead of the white fatsia seedheads shown here, or use gold candles and gold-sprayed berries at Thanksgiving.

The container for the decoration is a small antique wire basket with candle holders, and the container is lined firstly with moss and then with plastic. Any suitably raised container of a similar size would serve the purpose, such as a silver rose bowl, perhaps, or a plain china cake stand. You can use jars or eggcups to contain the candles and disguise them with moss.

▶ CLASSIC BY CANDLELIGHT
One of the key elements when creating a table centre decoration is to ensure that it is the right size and shape for the table. It should neither crowd the table nor look lost in the middle. It should also not be so tall that guests have to peer round it to talk to each other. At a smaller table the same style of arrangement should be created in a low, bowl-shaped container.

CREATING *the Festive Winter* TABLE SETTING

Finger-like fatsia leaves make a glossy base for this dome-shaped arrangement, with cones and seedheads adding height. In addition to the main table setting, simple individual decorations have been made from left-over foliage and bracken twigs.

INGREDIENTS

~

Fatsia leaves (Fatsia japonica)

Box (Buxus *sp.*)

Variegated holly (Ilex *sp.*)

Ivy (Hedera *sp.*)

Larch cones and twigs (Larix *sp.*)

Fir cones

Fatsia seedheads (Fatsia japonica)

~

Oasis

Plastic bin liner

Florist's wire

Candles

THE PROPORTIONS OF this table centre arrangement will depend on the size and shape of your container. The aim is to make a flat collar of foliage covering the rim of the container to surround the arrangement. You will, therefore, need a container that is fairly shallow, but it does need a foot, as the collar of leaves should hang below the base to look most effective. A flat cake stand would serve the purpose just as well as the wirework dish shown here; so would a rose bowl or shallow fruit dish with a short stem.

Any suitable mixture of evergreen leaves will work, provided you mix the textures and colours well, and the leaves are not too stiff.

Constructing the Table Setting

Fatsia seedheads
(FATSIA JAPONICA)

Ivy
(HEDERA *sp.*)

Variegated holly
(ILEX *sp.*)

Box
(BUXUS *sp.*)

Larch
cones & twigs
(LARIX *sp.*)

Fatsia leaves
(FATSIA JAPONICA)

Fir cone

1 *If the container is open-sided, first line it with moss. Then use a plastic bin liner, cut down, to provide a waterproof base. Pre-soak a block of wet oasis and place it on top of the plastic lining.*

2 *Into the sides of the container, insert the largest leaves, in this case fatsia, to create a collar covering the rim. Then insert the sprigs of box to make a second, slightly taller tier inside the first one.*

3 *Add the variegated holly and ivy in the centre, with the larch twigs at intervals between them. Wire two or three large cones and insert them, with some fatsia seedheads, in the centre of the arrangement. Finally place the candles in the candle holders.*

▲ LIGHT AND DARK

The combination of dark and variegated leaves, white seedheads and plain white candles creates an elegant centrepiece. When you see the leaves, seedheads and cones of this table centre arrangement in close up, you appreciate its textural qualities, and the contrasts of tone created by the dark foliage and the white candles. It is important when creating displays using a limited range of colours, like this one, to maximise contrasts of texture, form and tone to create the interest that would normally come from a richer colour mixture.

Constructing the Place Setting

1 *This simple small decoration is made from bracken stems, a few sprigs of box and one or two larch cones. Glue the bracken stems to a small cube of dry oasis. Trim them level once the glue is dry.*

2 *Insert the sprigs of box and the cones into the oasis, and finally tie with a couple of twists of gold braid, knotted to finish.*

CHRISTMAS FOLIAGE AND FRUIT GARLAND

Decking the halls with wreaths and garlands has a long tradition at Christmas.
A ready-made artificial garland can be quickly decorated with berries, cones, winter foliage,
fruit and ribbons to give a colourful welcome to visitors.

A SUITABLY FESTIVE mood at Christmas is instantly created if your first impression, as you walk into a room or hallway, is one of rich colours and scents. A garland draped over the banisters, a fireplace or even a doorway sets the mood perfectly.

A shop-bought undecorated garland made from artificial pine makes a quick and easy base to work from, although if you make your own there is nothing to beat the scent of fresh blue pine. Simply bind black plastic bin liners together with wire to form a thick sausage shape, and then wire the pieces of blue pine to the bin liner base to cover it.

Once you have fixed the garland in place by wiring it into position on the banister rail, or draping it over a mantelpiece or door architrave (fix a couple of nails into the architrave at each corner to hold it), you can decorate it as you please. If fixing a swag to a mantelpiece, always use a fireguard and be very careful not to create a fire hazard.

Garlands can be decorated with a range of fresh or dried materials, from pieces of evergreen foliage – ivy, holly and pine are particularly suitable – snipped from the garden, together with any brightly coloured berries you can find, such as cotoneaster or pyracantha. You can even use plastic berries: they look very realistic and will not dry out. Fresh fruit can be wired to the garland – including oranges, lemons and apples tied in bunches. Fir cones are ideal for adding bulk and scent. Dried orange or lemon slices, baked in a slow oven, then wired together in bunches, also make attractive Christmas garland decorations. Other appropriate additions include bunches of twigs and small terracotta pots filled with flowers or berries.

▶ **BANISTER GARLAND**
A small hallway, with a neutral colour scheme, is given a wonderfully festive treatment with this orange and red garland. Tartan ribbons, pyracantha berries in clusters of yellow and orange, and bright orange satsumas provide the colour notes on this otherwise plain and elegant foliage decoration.

▲ **FIREPLACE GARLAND**
This fireplace swag is the garland shown opposite with the more colourful decorations removed. The fir cones have been kept for their textural contrast. Always use a fireguard with such decorations to avoid fire hazard – the fireguard here was removed only briefly for the photograph. Whether you choose the plainer or more exuberant version depends on the décor and style of your house.

CREATING *the*
Christmas GARLAND

This garland is made from an artificial pine base, decorated with
foliage, fruit, fir cones, clay pots, bracken stems, ribbons and berries. It is fastened in
position on the banisters and decorated in situ.

To MAKE A Christmas garland, first decide where you are positioning it, and then estimate the length of base you need. A staircase garland can stretch all the way up one flight of stairs, for example, or simply cover the newel post, as you wish.

To work out the number of ingredients that you need to decorate the garland aim to have one large decoration – such as a big fir cone or large cluster of berries – spaced every six inches or so along the length, with the bunches of ivy and holly tied between.

If there are still sparse-looking areas, fill them in with extra satsumas or tartan ribbon tied in bows.

The decoration does not have to be symmetrical but you need to make sure that the items are spaced reasonably evenly along the length of the base – do not have all the berries crowded at one end for instance. The aim is to get a good balance of form, texture and colour throughout.

As this garland is to cover the length of the banister two artificial pine bases, 10ft (3m) long, were used.

INGREDIENTS
~
Synthetic pine garland base

Ivy (Hedera *sp.*)

Larch twigs and cones (Larix *sp.*)

Variegated holly (Ilex *sp.*)

Large pine cones

Red and yellow pyracantha berries
(Pyracantha *sp.*)

Satsumas

Dried bracken stems
~
Wired tartan ribbon

Terracotta pots, 4in (10cm) in diameter

Medium-gauge wire

Larch twigs
& cones
(LARIX *sp.*)

Ivy
(HEDERA *sp.*)

Variegated holly
(ILEX *sp.*)

synthetic pine garland

Red pyracantha
berries
(PYRACANTHA *sp.*)

Mature ivy
(HEDERA *sp.*)

Yellow
pyracantha
berries

Constructing the Garland

1 Fix the base to the newel post and drape it loosely along the banister rail, tying it at intervals with wire to create a snake-like effect.

2 Loosely drape the ivy over the garland base, tucking it in the garland to secure it. Some trailing stems can droop down attractively.

3 Flesh out the base by wiring the larch twigs, the bunches of ivy and the holly branches to it at intervals, to create a full, informal look.

Adding the Decoration

1 Add the cones and terracotta pots filled with pyracantha berries at regular intervals along the wreath. Check for any gaps in the garland, and fill with additional foliage or decorations, aiming to keep a balance of colour and form throughout the length of the garland.

2 Next add the bundles of bracken stems tied together with wired tartan ribbon (see page 123).

Terracotta pot

Dried bracken stems

Wired tartan ribbon

Pine cone

Satsuma

3 Finally wire the satsumas (see page 122) into any gaps where colour is needed, either singly or in pairs.

CHRISTMAS WINDOW WREATH

*A small wreath in the window at
Christmas is a welcoming seasonal touch
for this special time of year.*

AS AN ALTERNATIVE to a Christmas door
wreath, why not hang a wreath in the
window, Scandinavian-style? It is simple
enough for a child to make, and the slightly
irregular shape adds to its charm. For this
wreath, small ivy leaves were used to cover
the wire circle and dried cranberries for the
central star, but by all means experiment with
any materials you have to hand. White snow-
berries, plentiful at this time of year, would
look delicate, while yellow pyracantha berries
would make a splash of colour. The foliage
can be any small-leaved twining evergreen,
such as evergreen honeysuckle, for example.

Make a wire ring for the base. If you wrap
the wire around a large circular object (which
you remove afterwards) you can create a perfect
circle, but a slightly less regular shape, judged
by eye, looks just as effective.

To suspend the wreath, you will need to
create a wire loop, which can be covered in
ivy to disguise it, or you could hang the
wreath from a length of matching silk ribbon,
tied at the top with a neat bow.

▶ HANGING STAR
*This wreath looks just right in a small window, or in the
lower half of a larger window in which the blind is
lowered. Do not hang it alone in a vast window – it
will look lost. The light glancing through the leaves adds
to the charm but you can hang it on a door or wall if
you prefer, or simply suspend it from the ceiling.*

CREATING *the Christmas*
WINDOW WREATH

*To make this simple wreath to adorn your window, you first need
to construct a circular base for the ivy. Hang the star of dried cranberries, or
whatever berries you choose, onto the ivy ring.*

Dried cranberries

Ivy
(HEDERA sp.)

A VERY SIMPLE CIRCLE, made of heavy-duty florist's or garden wire, about 10in (25cm) in diameter, forms the base for this Swedish-inspired wreath. You will need some kind of evergreen twiner to wrap around the wire circle and some fine florist's wire to bind it on to the base with. The dried cranberries can be obtained from any good supermarket in the weeks before Christmas, or you can use any other coloured berries that you might have in the garden – holly berries, for example.

1 *To make the star, first cut a long length of medium-gauge florist's wire about two and a half times as long as the chosen diameter of the star from tip to tip. Thread the cranberries onto the wire.*

2 *When you have enough cranberries threaded, shape the wire into a five-sided star; it does not have to be perfectly symmetrical. Clip off any surplus wire and bind the ends together with fine wire to close it.*

3 *Form the heavy-duty wire into a circular shape, either by hand or by wrapping it round a circular object. Wind fine wire around the join.*

4 *Prepare the stems of ivy and begin by laying one along the circular base. Holding it in place, wind fine florist's wire around it to secure it.*

5 *Continue in this way using several layers of ivy stems to hide the wire. Suspend the star from the base with a small wire hook.*

Christmas Window Tree Alternative

*This miniature tree can be positioned in front of a window
where it will catch the light. Spraying some of the decorations gold or silver
creates additional sparkle.*

F OR THIS IMITATION Christmas tree, a wicker basket was filled with dry oasis, twiggy bare branches inserted into it, and variegated holly and ivy used to disguise the oasis base. The branches were then hung with small home-made decorations – dried orange slices, sprayed cones and fruit, tiny

pomanders (see pages 108-110), little hearts made of dried cranberries and miniature baskets of roses, as well as circles of birch twigs. Your choice of decoration depends on what is available in the house. Try to keep the colour theme simple – this one centres on golds, oranges and rust colours.

▼ **FESTOONED TWIGS**
This 'tree' is about 3ft (90cm) tall. You can make a larger or smaller version, but keep the decorations in scale with the twiggy branches as here. They will also need to be quite light or the branches will bow down with the weight. Foil-wrapped sweets could be used for a child's party tree.

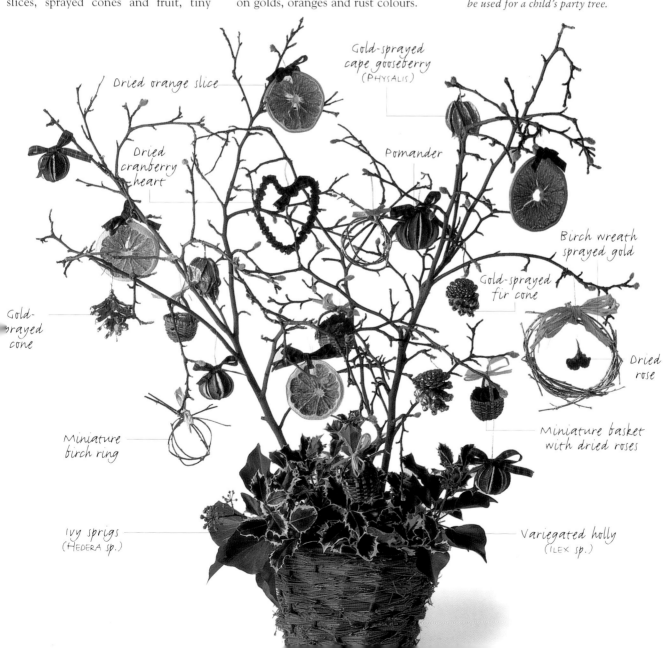

Gold-sprayed
cape gooseberry
(PHYSALIS)

Dried orange slice

Dried
cranberry
heart

Pomander

Birch wreath
sprayed gold

Gold-sprayed
fir cone

Gold-
sprayed
cone

Dried
rose

Miniature
birch ring

Miniature basket
with dried roses

Ivy sprigs
(HEDERA sp.)

Variegated holly
(ILEX sp.)

Scent around the HOUSE

WHAT COULD be more welcoming than the scent of lilies or roses wafting through the house on a summer's evening? There are scented flowers for all seasons – in winter witch-hazel or daphne will fill a room with fragrance and so will bowls of aromatic pot-pourri.

DISPLAYING SCENTED SPRING BULBS

Scented bulbs are a real bonus in late winter and early spring, their rich colours and wonderfully pervasive scent bringing life and colour to the house at a time of year when there is relatively little in the way of flowering plants. Support bulbs carefully to keep them blooming as long as possible.

Grape
hyacinth
(MUSCARI
ARMENIACUM)

◀ MUSCARI BULBS

Grape hyacinth (Muscari) bulbs are delicate flowers with a striking depth of blue that is seen to best advantage when the flowers are gathered en masse. Some varieties such as Muscari armeniacum have a delicate scent, best appreciated indoors. The blue-patterned soup tureen used here echoes the blue of the flowers and allows plenty of space to hide an unattractive plastic pot. A layer of moss is added to conceal bare soil and to give the appearance of a natural setting.

▶ PUSSY WILLOW BASKET

Hyacinths are among the first signs of a new season of growth and fill the air with their sweet scent. The pots are placed inside a wicker basket which is then covered with ivy, moss and fungus, giving the impression of a woodland glade. Take care when you make the cage of twigs that the proportions are appropriate to the height of the flowers – about half as tall again as the tallest flowers looks about right.

IN SPRING, YOU have a wide choice of bulbs for the house which are mostly forced so that they come out earlier than garden bulbs. They bring a welcome foretaste of spring to your rooms well before spring actually arrives. Among the best scented bulbs are daffodils and hyacinths; others, such as some types of grape hyacinth, are equally attractive but are less strongly scented.

Pretty though the larger bulbs are, they often droop in the warmth of room. They are best kept in as cool an environment as possible until the buds are ready to open and when brought into warmth should be given some additional support. Finding ways to provide this without interfering with the delicate appearance of the bulbs and thereby spoiling the display is an art in itself.

There are many different forms of support or frame you can use, but the most attractive are those that complement the plants. These you can make yourself from nature's own materials – twisted twigs or the supple stems of trees or shrubs are ideal for the purpose.

A container that disguises the plastic pot in which the bulbs are normally supplied is an important element in the overall effect. You can use a ceramic cachepot or a basket lined with plastic. Moss is an excellent material for covering the unattractive bare soil in the pot and also conserves moisture.

After flowering the bulbs should be allowed to die down naturally. When the foliage has withered, lift the bulbs and store them in a cool, dry, dark place for replanting in the autumn. Alternatively, plant them out in the garden after flowering.

If you wish, you can group several small containers of bulbs, scented and unscented, on a kitchen window-sill or occasional table. Keep the colours to a limited range – blues and yellows, perhaps – for the best effect.

MAKING A *Pussy Willow* BASKET

Some flowering bulbs, notably hyacinths, daffodils and freesias, flop unattractively
once they are in full flower. Since shop-bought supports, such as green plastic rings, are extremely
ugly, why not make a caged support out of a sympathetic natural material?

TO MAKE THE pussy willow cage you will need eight stems of pussy willow for a container about 10in (25cm) in diameter. This kind of support works best over a group of hyacinths; construct it just before the hyacinths are in flower.

INGREDIENTS
~
Bowl of Dutch hyacinths
(Hyacinthus orientalis)

Pussy willow (Salix caprea)

Moss

Ivy (Hedera *sp.*)

Fungus or bark
~
Raffia

Raffia

Pussy willow
(SALIX CAPREA)

Dutch
hyacinth bulb
(HYACINTHUS ORIENTALIS)

Ivy
(HEDERA
HELIX *sp.*)

Moss   Fungus

1 *Cut the branches so that each one measures twice the height of the tallest flowers. Insert the base of each stem at regular intervals around the edge of the container.*

2 *Decorate the base of the container with moss, a few ivy leaves and some fungus or whatever sympathetic material you may have to hand – fir cones, perhaps, or pieces of bark.*

3 *Twist the ends of the opposite pairs of branches over each other, tucking any stray ends in as neatly as you can. Take care not to snap the branches – handle them carefully.*

4 *To maintain the natural theme, tie the branches at the top using several pieces of raffia secured in a simple knot, to hold the top tightly in place.*

Willow Twig Alternative

This simple willow twig frame is ideal for keeping the narcissus flowers upright.

TALL NARCISSUS FLOWERS will often need some support once the flowers have opened. You can create a circular hedge of twisted willow stems (*Salix matsudana* 'Tortuosa') to provide the support for the flowers. You will need a dozen or so stems, cut to a few inches taller than the flowers. Hide the narcissus container in an attractive ceramic cachepot and fill the gap between the two with dry oasis, which will provide a support for the willow 'hedge'. A collar of green moss is then inserted into the oasis between the pot of narcissus and the rim of the china bowl for a natural effect. Alternatively, if there is enough room, you can insert the willow twigs directly into the bulb container, being very careful not to damage the bulbs themselves.

NARCISSUS AND WILLOW

Tall narcissus will often need some support once the flowers open. You can create an attractive circular 'hedge' of twisted willow stems (Salix matsudana 'Tortuosa') to provide support for them. You will need a dozen or so stems to surround a fairly large bowl of bulbs. Cut them down so that they are just a few inches longer than the flowers themselves and insert the bases of the stems either into the oasis or, if you have room, directly into the edge of the compost around the bulbs.

For this display, a blue and white china tureen forms the cachepot for the plastic pot of narcissus. The moss serves to disguise the original container and the oasis.

Twisted willow
(SALIX MATSUDANA 'Tortuosa')

Narcissus
(NARCISSUS 'Cheerfulness')

Woodland moss

COUNTRY LAVENDER

Lavender has noted soothing properties, and is ideal for creating a mood of tranquility. Simple yet elegant, it suits both sophisticated and country-style interiors.

◄ **LAVENDER AND ROSE BASKET** ►
The lavender basket sits well on a dresser with blue and white china. The heads of lavender will scent the room delightfully for several months. The close-up picture of the basket on the right illustrates the exceptionally good colour of this variety of lavender (Lavandula angustifolia *'Hidcote').*

LAVENDER IS ONE of the most pungently fragrant of all herbs and it retains its scent when dry, which is why is is so often used in sachets and pot-pourri. A container filled with sweet-smelling herbs gives any room a welcoming feel. This basket, made with fresh and dried flowers and filled with fresh lavender heads, will dry *in situ*, retaining its scent for many months. Although all lavender is aromatic, some forms have a stronger perfume and are more brilliantly coloured than others – *Lavandula angustifolia* 'Hidcote' is particularly good in both respects and is well worth hunting out to plant in your garden. The deep colour will remain vivid even when the lavender dries. If you are not able to pick fresh flowers, you can equally well use dried lavender for this bowl.

A small wicker basket is a perfect container for lavender. The one shown here is about 7in (18cm) in diameter and is small enough to sit comfortably on a dresser.

CREATING *the Lavender and Rose* BASKET

This basket is very simple to make and lasts over an exceptionally long period as the lavender will dry in situ. *You will need a plentiful supply of fresh or dried lavender, and a few roses to make it.*

THIS SIMPLE DECORATED basket, filled with lavender flower heads, could serve as the blueprint for many other similar baskets. You could, for example, use crossed bunches of herbs instead of lavender, and fill the middle with chopped herbs, to act as the centrepiece for a dinner party (particularly if you are serving pasta – the guests can then add their own herbs).

To make sure the final effect is neat, you will need to ensure that the crossed bunches of lavender heads are all roughly the same length. Select the stems of lavender, hold the heads upside down and tap them gently on the worksurface to level them, and then snip the stems about 6in (15cm) from the heads. This ensures the bunches are full and the heads evenly spaced and distributed.

INGREDIENTS

~

Lavender
(Lavandula angustifolia '*Hidcote*')

Moss

Dried Roses (Rosa)

~

Medium-gauge florist's wire

Rose
(ROSA)

Lavender
(LAVANDULA ANGUSTIFOLIA
'Hidcote')

Moss

1 *Bind moss to the edge of the basket using florist's wire. This provides a base for the crossed lavender bundles and disguises the basket's edge.*

2 *Bind about 15 stems together for each bunch of lavender. Then arrange the bunches in crossed pairs around the rim of the container.*

3 *Into the centre of each crossed pair of lavender bunches, insert a rose. Wire the rose into the basket to secure it (see page 123).*

4 *Fill the centre of the basket with broken stems and heads of lavender. If necessary, fill the base with moss before adding the heads.*

Alternative Lavender Arrangement

*If you do not want to go to the trouble of making a
lavender pot-pourri basket, but enjoy the scent of lavender, this simple
trug of lavender and roses smells equally good.*

LAVENDER HAS a wonderfully nostalgic scent, and it is also a well-known relaxant, used widely nowadays in aromatherapy. What could be more restful than the delicious scent of lavender in the bedroom? This small trug of lavender and roses can be made from dry or fresh flowers, as you prefer, and it will last for many months, scenting the room delightfully.

If you have plenty of lavender stems, fill the base of the trug with moss, then place the lavender heads at each end, the stems pointing towards the centre of the trug. Fill the centre with a couple of rows of roses. Alternatively, if you have only a few heads of lavender, and some roses, you could fill a small trug with pot-pourri and strew the lavender and roses over the top. Bind the handle and the sides of the trug with hops or a similar vine to give it a country look.

Other flowers that will look good with lavender include small bright gold marigolds – their heads can be used in the same way as the roses to create neat, symmetrical rows in a contrasting display. You could also use pink and blue cornflowers, for a softer, more harmonious colour scheme.

◄ **TRUG ARRANGEMENT**
A small, hand-made wooden trug or an oval or rectangular wicker basket filled with scented old-fashioned cottage flowers, like these rows of lavender and roses, makes the ideal arrangement for a simple country bedroom. You can vary the additional contents of the trug to match the colour scheme of the room.

GARDEN ROSES ARRANGEMENT

Classical in their simplicity, and with an exquisite scent, garden roses look best when simply arranged either on their own or with just one other kind of flower.

◄ ROSES ►
The traditional charm of garden roses is ideally suited to a well-appointed drawing room. They provide not only sweet fragrance but delicate colour too. The velvety petals of roses have a fresh, unsophisticated appeal, matched by the prettily patterned china. A few sprigs of lady's mantle bulk out the arrangement.

SCENTED FLOWERS ARE a great joy in the house. They fill rooms with their perfume, adding a feeling of calm and tranquillity. Roses are probably the best known, and some of the most highly scented, flowers for this purpose, but there are plenty of others, too. Armfuls of lilac, simple twigs of witch hazel in the winter, bowls of lilies or hyacinths, all play a similar role.

The secret is to create very simple arrangements in suitably matched containers. Roses look good in jugs, in tankards and in silver punch bowls. Lilac, being larger, can be gathered into a large ceramic wash-jug. A few stems of witch hazel can take on a Japanese look in a simple plain earthenware vase.

If you have a garden, you should be able to grow something scented for every season – daffodils or hyacinths in spring, viburnum or lilac in early summer, roses and lilies in midsummer, Mexican orange (*Choisya ternata*) foliage in autumn and witch hazel or some types of daphne in winter.

CREATING *the Garden Roses* ARRANGEMENT

Easy to put together, this arrangement of sumptuous roses needs only a fairly narrow necked container and some scrunched-up chicken wire to support the stems of the roses.

THIS SIMPLY constructed arrangement can be made from any garden roses you have, together with a few sprigs of subtle, soft-textured flowers, such as lady's mantle, that are available at the same time of year. Failing these, use any good light-coloured garden foliage with small leaves. You will need to form a loose ball of chicken wire to fit the neck of the jug you use – 1in (2.5cm) gauge chicken wire is ideal.

The roses will need preparation – crush the stems and strip off lower leaves to make the flowers last.

ROSA
'Chapeau de Napoléon'

Lady's mantle
(ALCHEMILLA MOLLIS)

ROSA
'Duc de Guiche'

ROSA
'Dublin Bay'

ROSA
'Celsiana'

1 *Fill the pot with water. Cut chicken wire about an inch larger all round than the neck of the jug, and push it into the jug, forming a dome shape.*

2 *Build a frame of the additional flower or foliage material (in this case lady's mantle) to create a collar around the jug.*

3 *Cut the stems of the roses at an angle and crush the base of the stems with a hammer. Strip any leaves that will be below the water-line.*

4 *Insert the roses, evenly spaced, in the centre of the arrangement, trimming them if necessary to create an evenly shaped dome.*

Alternative Scented Arrangement

*Using silvery senecio foliage instead of lady's mantle as a foil to
the blooms, and choosing just one type of peony, you can create a similarly
beautifully scented, yet equally simple, arrangement.*

SIMPLE JUGS OF large scented flowers have long been used to create a welcoming atmosphere in the home, and are much better suited to the decor of most people's houses than formally constructed arrangements. The beauty of the flowers is all the more evident when they are displayed alone or with a few stems of attractive foliage.

Simple though the arrangement is, you need to ensure that the proportions are appropriate and the forms of container and flowers are well matched. The arrangement should not dwarf the container, or vice versa. For a natural-looking arrangement, let the flowers spread out widthways, so that they do not look rigidly bunched in the container. It is better to use few flowers, with a little foliage, than cram them tightly into the vase or jug.

Peony
(PAEONIA sp.)

senecio
(BRACHYGLOTTIS
GREYI)

▶ GREY AND WHITE
Large, blowzy peony flowers combine well here with the soft silvery-grey felted leaves of senecio, but in summer there is a wide range of other foliage to choose from. Woody stems (of both foliage and flowers) will need to be crushed first to allow them to take up water (see page 117).

POMANDER AND POT-POURRI

These scented room sweeteners, created from flower petals, fruit
and spices, have a long history in the home and repay the small effort they demand
with wonderful scents over a long period of time.

A CENTURY AGO no self-respecting bourgeois housewife would have dreamed of being without a few bowls of pot-pourri scattered around the house, or the odd pomander to scent the linen cupboard. It is well worth reviving this ancient craft for the sheer delight you will get from the subtle fragrances they release over a long period of time. Pot-pourri can be made from the petals of any scented flowers, with the addition of scented pieces of bark, such as cinnamon, if you wish. Pomanders are a little more time-consuming to create but will last almost indefinitely. You will need some sound fruit and a good supply of aromatic cloves to make them.

In addition to making pomanders out of clove-studded fruit, you can create equally aromatic ones from short sprigs of rosemary, packed tightly together to stud a ball of dry oasis. They will bring a spicy and long-lasting fragrance to a room. Instead of hanging them up, you can make several and display them in a shallow china or glass bowl on a low table or bedside cabinet.

◄ **POT-POURRI**
A pretty china bowl is the obvious choice of container for a summery pot-pourri made from mixed scented flower petals, primarily roses and lavender.

POMANDER ►
Hanging pomanders in the linen cupboard not only imparts a delicious scent to the linen, but also deters flying pests, such as moths. With their neat, almost sculptural, form and interesting texture, pomanders also make an attractive decoration in their own right, grouped in an elegant glass or china bowl.

CREATING *the Clove* POMANDER

You need a few firm, sound fruits, such as oranges,
limes or lemons and a good supply of cloves, plus a small quantity of 'curing'
spices in which the pomander dries.

THE SHAPE AND form of your pomander will depend on the fruit you choose as the base. Citrus fruits tend to be used most often, as they add a delicious scent of their own to that of the cloves. Oranges, lemons, grapefruit, limes and even kumquats are all suitable. Use good quality cloves with sound 'heads'. You can then decorate the fruit as you wish – either by completely covering it with cloves, or by arranging the cloves in rows or a more elaborate pattern. If you want to hang the pomander, it is a good idea to divide the fruit into quarters with florist's tape, leaving these areas unstudded with cloves. When the rest of the fruit is covered with cloves, mix the spices below in a bowl. Roll the fruit in the spices and decant the fruit and spices into a brown paper bag. Leave for two weeks. Then remove the florist's tape and tie the fruit with narrow coloured ribbon or gold cord.

Covering the fruit with cloves is a tricky business. If the skin is hard, pierce it with a nail or darning needle before you insert each clove, but with softer-skinned fruit, you can push the clove directly into the fruit skin.

1 *To create a space to tie a ribbon around the pomander, quarter the fruit using florist's tape. Discard any cloves that have broken seedheads.*

2 *Using the tape as a guide, insert the cloves in neat rows. Make sure each clove is pushed down firmly and evenly up to the shaft.*

Orange
Ribbon
Ground cloves
Ground nutmeg
Whole cloves
Orris root
Ground cinnamon
Ground allspice

INGREDIENTS

~

Orange

Whole cloves

Ground cloves

Ground nutmeg

Ground cinnamon

Ground allspice

Orris root

~

Ribbon

3 *Work your way around the fruit, filling each quarter segment as you work. When you are finished, remove the tape and put the fruit in a brown paper bag filled with the spices.*

CREATING *the Scented* POT-POURRI

Pot-pourri, using dried flowers and herbs,
has been a favoured way of scenting rooms for centuries, long before
air-fresheners were invented.

THE RECIPE for pot-pourri here relies primarily on lavender, roses and marjoram for scent, with the addition of a few 'pretty' petals to add colour and texture to the mixture. The addition of a small quantity of orris root (bought in good chemist's shops or flower suppliers) 'cures' the mixture and ensures it stays fresh. Use only freshly harvested petals that are totally dry when picked. Break the flowerheads into petals, place in a paper bag, add the orris root and store in a dark place for 2 weeks, turning the mixture occasionally.

> ### INGREDIENTS
> ~
> *Lavender*
> *Rose petals*
> *Roses*
> *Larkspur florets*
> *Dried dahlias*
> *Orris root*
> *Marjoram*
> *Statice*

Dried dahlia

Rose petals

Orris root

Larkspur florets

Lavender

Rose petals

Roses

Marjoram

Roses

Statice

Lavender Balls

These little lavender balls make a wonderfully simple
and fragrant alternative to the clove pomander.

USING A SMALL ball of dry oasis and the broken flowerheads of lavender, you can create wonderfully scented, attractive lavender balls to hang in a linen cupboard.

▶ **CREATING THE LAVENDER BALL**
Cover a ball of oasis in glue and roll it in a dish of lavender heads. When dry, tie a coloured ribbon round the ball.

Equipment
and
TECHNIQUES

ALL SUCCESSFUL floral decorators are well versed in the basic tricks of the trade. This chapter shows you the basic equipment required and provides a simple course in essential skills, from conditioning fresh flowers to wiring dried ones.

EQUIPMENT AND TECHNIQUES

*Creating fresh and dried flower arrangements demands relatively
little skill but there are a few useful pieces of equipment, and some simple tips and techniques
applicable to many kinds of arrangement.*

YOU WILL NEED a reasonably large work space for creating
flower arrangements. For fresh flowers, you should be
within easy reach of a water supply. Make sure you have good
light to work in and a bin or bin-liner for waste materials.

To make your preparation easier, you should ideally keep
any equipment that you use regularly – such as a sharp knife,
scissors, oasis and wires – in a handy portable container with
compartments.

Try to assemble all the materials and do any preliminary
work – preparing stems, trimming leaves and wiring bunches
for example – in advance of the actual arranging so that your
work flows smoothly.

Remember that it pays to put your arrangement into its
position in the final stages. That way you will be able to
adjust the shape to where it will actually be seen and also to
fill any holes and gaps that become obvious once it is in the
right place. Arrangements that are above the normal sight
line may need some filling in around the base of the arrangement, and those you look down on – such as low displays on
coffee tables – will need checking to ensure the mechanics of
supporting the arrangement are not visible.

▶ GETTING PREPARED

*A kitchen or study table makes a suitable work station for preparing
and arranging flowers, provided you have storage space nearby to
keep your essential equipment. Use a cutting board when trimming
stems or cutting oasis to fit a container and make sure any scissors
and knives are really sharp. Store equipment neatly when not in use.*

Fresh Flower Equipment

Wire wreath base · Oasis tray · Oasis bowl · Florist's tape · Knife · Florist's wires · Chicken wire · Oasis tape · Scissors · Bowl · String · Rope · Raffia · Ribbon · Oasis foam ball · Oasis foam brick · Oasis spike or 'frog' · Florist's wire · Rubber bands · Glass marbles · Long pins · Reel wire · Oasis foam ring · Oasis pins

Dried Flower Equipment

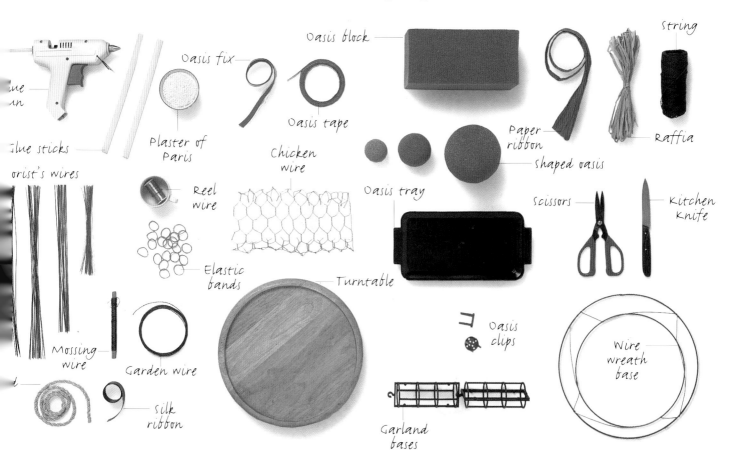

Glue gun

Glue sticks

Florist's wires

Plaster of Paris

Oasis fix

Oasis tape

Reel wire

Chicken wire

Oasis block

Oasis tray

Paper ribbon

String

Raffia

Shaped oasis

Scissors

Kitchen Knife

Elastic bands

Turntable

Mossing wire

Garden wire

Oasis clips

Wire wreath base

Silk ribbon

Garland bases

FRESH AND DRIED FLOWER TECHNIQUES

*Learning a few simple tips will give your flower
arrangements, whether fresh or dried, the professional finish that makes
all the difference to their success.*

THE TECHNIQUES YOU use for fresh and dried flowers are different because of the nature of the materials. The chief aim with fresh flowers is to keep them alive and at the peak of their health for as long as you possibly can. With dried flowers, which are naturally brittle, your main aim is to prevent the stems from breaking and to support them as required for the display you want to achieve.

There are just a few basic techniques for both fresh and dried flowers that you will find are universal to most arrangements. Once you have put these techniques into practice a few times with fresh or dried flowers you will quickly master them so that they become almost second-nature.

Most professional florists work very fast. To do so, they make sure that they have the right equipment to hand and organize themselves well in advance. They also work only with the finest materials. It is very important to find a good supplier of fresh or well-dried flowers. Your arrangements depend for their beauty on the best possible flowers. It may be worth your while to form a flower club with a few friends so that you can buy in bulk from a wholesaler.

Fresh Flower Techniques

FRESH FLOWERS HAVE only an ephemeral beauty but they will last a great deal longer if you treat them with respect and remember that, even though cut, they are still living things. If they are to retain their freshness it is important not to subject them to over-heating, either from radiators or brilliant sunshine; they will last a great deal longer in cool temperatures, which is why florist's shops are so cold!

In centrally heated houses, you do not have a great deal of choice about the ambient temperature, but select the coolest place that you can and, before you arrange the flowers, gradually acclimatize them so they do not suffer from a sudden change of temperature.

If you are buying fresh flowers, check their condition first. Not all florists are reputable, and some flowers may be well past their best. The foliage should look fresh and bright, not wilted or yellowing. Flowerheads should either be in bud or just starting to open. Chrysanthemum flowers should have a tighly packed centre of stamens; once the stamens start to splay out, the flowers are past their peak.

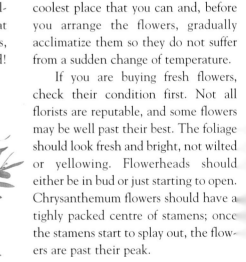

◄ FRESH FLOWERS
*Place all purchased cut flowers in a bucket
of cold water for a good hour before
arranging them. Woody stems need extra
attention to increase the take-up of water.
Slicing or hammering the stems to increase
the cut surface helps; so does the hot and
cold water treatment shown opposite.*

Preparing flowers

ALL FLOWERS need some preparation before they can be used in flower arrangement to ensure that the flowers look their best for as long as possible. You can even refresh flowers that have wilted from lack of water. Make sure that the water you use is fresh, and that you change the water for fresh flowers regularly, ideally every other day.

CONDITIONING FLOWERS
Most fresh flowers need some conditioning before being arranged. The techniques that you use will depend to some extent on the kind of flower, and the condition they are in when you buy them. Always aim to purchase flowers that are obviously in good condition, and do not leave them too long out of water.

HOT AND COLD WATER TREATMENT
Woody-stemmed flowers can benefit from a shock to release any air lock in the stem. Fill a bucket with hot, not boiling water, and plunge the flowers in this for 10 seconds or so before returning them to fresh cold water.

REFRESHING FLOWERS
To refresh flowers that have suffered a serious lack of water but are not permanently damaged, remove any extra foliage and plunge the stems into cold water. After about half an hour the plant's stem will become erect and the flowers will lift into their normal position. The heads of wilting florist's roses can be revived by cutting the stems and putting them in hot water for a few minutes to release the air lock and then putting them in cold water for a long drink.

REMOVING LEAVES
If you allow leaves to remain on the stems below the water-line of the vase or container, they will taint the water, make the water smell and cause the whole plant to die more rapidly. Remove any lower leaves where they might be in contact with the water before assembling arrangements.

CRUSHING STEMS
Fibrous and woody stemmed plants, such as roses and viburnum, will need to have their stems crushed in order to increase the take-up of water. Cut the stems down to the length required and then lay them on a chopping board before hammering the last 1in (2.5cm) of stem to crush the bark. Normally one blow with the hammer is sufficient for the purpose. Bear in mind that crushed stems cannot be inserted into oasis and you will instead need a framework of chicken wire to hold the arrangement in place.

Enhancing fresh flowers

YOU WILL SOMETIMES need to prepare fresh flowers in certain ways before they are used in order to improve their appearance and ensure that they appear at their best in the arrangement. There are various tips and techniques for the purpose, depending on the kind of flowers you are using. Here are some of the more useful preparation techniques.

CUTTING OFF DEAD OR DAMAGED FLOWERS

Flowers with spires of flowerheads, such as freesias or gladioli, come out in succession, the base flowers dying off as the upper buds open. It is a good idea to remove any of the base blooms that are past their best; this will not only improve the appearance but prolong the life of the flowers.

WIRING SOFT STEMS

Some flowers with large flowerheads and slightly soft, sappy stems may droop unattractively, as the weight of the flowers is too great for the strength of the stem. Gerberas, for example, often present this kind of problem. The solution is to wire the stems with medium-gauge green wire. Push the wire through the centre of the flowerhead and out at the base (top left). Leave a short piece of wire protruding and loop this short end into a hook shape. Twist the long piece of wire gently, and not too tightly, down the length of the stem.

REMOVING LEAVES TO REVEAL FRUIT

Plants chosen for their colourful berries may well also be covered in less than attractive leaves. To allow the fruit to take centre stage in its full glory, snip off any unwanted leaves using a sharp pair of scissors.

REMOVING STAMENS

Some flowers, such as lilies, have stamens covered in pollen which can stain hands or clothes. The stamens may also stain the petals of the flowers unattractively. Using a tissue if necessary, separate the stamens and snip off at the base with a sharp pair of scissors.

OPENING CLOSED BUDS

Sometimes flowers are insufficiently opened to look at their best in an arrangement that is needed in time for a special occasion. Florists will normally gently tease such buds out by hand, to persuade the full flowers to be revealed. If you attempt to do this, you must carry out this procedure with the utmost care, as it is only too easy to damage the flowers beyond repair. Irises will respond easily to being treated in this way but again you must handle the flowers with the greatest care so as not to bruise or tear the delicate petals.

Using Pot-grown Plants

POT-GROWN PLANTS are particularly useful as they last so much longer than cut flowers. However, the pots in which they are grown are usually unattractive plastic and you will prefer to create displays using more attractive containers. Pot-grown plants in particular usually look best removed from their plastic pots and combined in a single container. It is useful occasionally to use non-waterproof containers for flowers and plants, and these will need lining. A cut down plastic bin liner is ideal unless you already have sheets of polythene to use for the purpose. To cover the soil at the top of the plants,

use moss (available from any good garden centre or florist). A little gravel in the base of the liner will help to improve drainage and stop the plants becoming waterlogged.

Once the flowering display of pot plants is past its best, you can transfer any bulbs to a bed or border in the garden once all danger of frost has passed. If there is a large difference in temperature between indoors and outdoors, acclimatize the plants by putting them outside only in the day time for a couple of days, bringing them in at night, before planting them up in the soil.

Bin liner

Moss

Gravel chips

MATERIALS FOR LINING A BASKET
You will need a plastic liner – use either a cut down bin-liner or polythene. You will also need some gravel chips to insert in the base of the liner, and a quantity of fresh sphaghnum moss to disguise the compost and give a pretty woodland effect.

LINING A BASKET
Line the base and sides of the basket with the spaghnum moss, forming a collar of moss at the rim of the basket. Then cut down the bin liner to the shape required to fit the basket and insert it into the base of the basket. Finally cover the base of the liner with a generous layer of gravel chips to improve drainage.

REMOVING PLANT FROM POT

If the plant is firmly wedged into its pot, tap the base hard on a flat surface and then, turning the plant upside down, gently draw the plant out from the pot. If the plant is well and truly wedged in the pot, you may have to cut the pot away using garden scissors.

Dwarf daffodil
(NARCISSUS sp.)

Primula hybrid
(PRIMULA)

▶ FRESH FLOWERS
Little pots of primulas and dwarf daffodils fill this woven basket, lined with plastic. If you keep the display moist, it will last far longer than a fresh flower display.

Dried Flower Techniques

Y OU CAN USE a variety of bought dried flowers and attractive seedheads from a good florist's shop or garden centre, but they can be quite expensive. Alternatively, you can dry your own quite easily, provided that you have enough space to do so. You will need a rack in a reasonably cool, dry room from which to hang the bunches of flowers. It is best to keep the flowers out of bright, direct sunlight as this can bleach and fade their colour while they are drying. Make sure that there is a good air flow so the air can circulate well round the flowers. In a damp or stuffy room the bunches may well become mouldy before they have had a chance to dry out completely.

How to dry flowers

E NSURE THAT YOU pick the flowers when they are dry – ideally after any dew has evaporated but before the hottest time of day. You must then bunch the flowers carefully, taking care not to damage or snap the stems.

Rubber bands can be used to hold the bunch in place as the stems will shrink when they dry. You also need to wire the bunches after they have been bunched, so that you can hang them, upside down, from the drying rack.

BUNCHING UP FRESH FLOWERS FOR DRYING
Remove any dead or damaged stems first and make a bunch of a dozen or so good quality blooms. Then fasten the stems together using an elastic band. Finally, wire the stems, leaving a long tail of wire to serve as a hanging loop.

STORING DRIED FLOWERS
Once the flowers are thoroughly dry – which may take up to three weeks – lay the flowers, head to toe in alternate layers, in a box lined with tissue paper.

▶ **HANGING DRYING FLOWERS**
A rack of freshly picked flowers hangs in an airy kitchen. The rack is sufficiently attractive to make a decorative feature, especially if you hang a few baskets or straw hats from it in addition to the flowers. Try to adjust the flowers on the rack so that the heads are at different levels by using wire hooks of differing lengths. This allows the air to circulate more freely, which will dry the flowers more quickly.

Wiring and drying techniques

MANY DRIED FLOWER arrangements rely heavily for their lavish appearance on wire supports for the flowers, since the stems are often brittle. More interesting and textural arrangements can be created if you use fruits and fir cones as well as flowers, and these will need to be wired so that they can be positioned precisely where they are needed. Finally, additional decorations can be created with some simple techniques – a bunch of twigs or spicy cinnamon sticks can be wired and tied with a coloured ribbon appropriate to the season or occasion. Fresh fruit can be sliced, dried in the oven and then wired to attach to a garland or Christmas tree, for example.

Wiring is a very simple technique to master. Do not use a heavy hand and make sure that you do not overwire. Use a short length of fine rose wire for delicate bunches; thicker stems may need medium-gauge wire. A couple of twists are all that is required to hold most dried flowers in place. Beginners tend to over-egg the pudding, making numerous twists of wire 'for safety', which not only takes longer, but often breaks or spoils the dried flowers.

WIRING UP FRESH FLOWERS FOR DRYING

Lay the wire over the stem, holding it in place with your thumb, with a short end protruding on one side. Wind the longer end around the stem twice, and leave the long tail of wire protruding. This is used to fix the bunch into the arrangement.

WIRING FRUIT

Take the fruit and pierce it through the bottom third with a length of medium-gauge wire, so that the wire runs right through the fruit and out the other side. One end of the wire should be about three times the length of the other protruding end. Then twist the long end a couple of times over the shorter end to secure.

MAKING ORANGE SLICES

Orange (or lemon) slices make deliciously scented decorations for garlands and wreaths. Slice the fruit quite thinly and lay the slices on a baking tray. Smaller fruit, such as clementines, can be left whole but with the skin cut into eighths. Put the fruit on the tray and bake in a very low oven for a couple of hours. Place fruit slices in a warm place such as an airing cupboard or on top of a boiler for about one week, turning occasionally. Spray the fruit with gloss varnish and allow it to dry. Wire several rings together to make a bunch and open out to make a fan shape.

WIRING CLAY POTS

Clay pots make a handsome addition to many floral decorations. Insert a wire through the pot and the drainage hole. Twist the ends together at the rim, leaving a long tail. Insert a second wire underneath the first at the base and twist it to secure. Tuck the short end into the drainage hole to stop the wire moving. The long end provides the second anchor wire.

WIRING CONES

Fir cones are wonderfully scented and highly textural and come in many shapes and sizes. To wire them you will need to pass a medium-gauge wire around the scales of the cone just above the base. Push the wire around the cone, leaving a short length protruding, and twist the longer end round the shorter end to secure.

WIRING TWIGS

Bunch the twigs together with a rubber band. Twist medium-gauge wire a couple of times round the centre of the bundle, leaving a long tail.

TYING A BOW

A ribbon bow adds a decorative finish to a bunch of cinnamon sticks and you can use tartan for a seasonal effect or a colour that ties in with the wreath or garland you are making. The best effect is achieved by using wire-edged ribbon as it holds its shape without flopping. Firstly, knot the ribbon round the bundle of cinnamon sticks in the usual way and then push the ribbon tails up to give the effect of ribbon loops, using the wired ribbon to keep the shape.

WIRING DRIED FRUIT

Slices of dried fruit look very attractive wired in bunches of several rings of fruit together, using medium gauge wire. To add the finishing touch, simply wrap a small ribbon round the wire and tie in a neat bow.

FLOWER LISTING

Whether you want to create arrangements to scent your home, to provide a complement
or contrast to the colour scheme of a room, or grow plants in your garden that will provide a year-round
supply of ingredients, these suggestions will help.

SCENTED PLANTS

Broom (*Genista* sp.)
Carnation/pink (*Dianthus* sp.)
Christmas box (*Sarcococca* sp.)
Freesia (*Freesia* sp.)
Honeysuckle (*Lonicera* sp. – most)
Hyacinth (*Hyacinthus orientalis*)
Lavender (*Lavandula angustifolia, L. spica*)
Lilac (*Syringa* sp.)
Lily (*Lilium* sp.)
Mimosa (*Acacia dealbata*)
Mock orange blossom (*Philadelphus* sp.)
Myrtle (*Myrtus communis*)
Narcissus (*Narcissus* sp. – many)
Rose (*Rosa* sp. – many)
Scented geranium (*Pelargonium tomentosum*)
Sweet pea (*Lathyrus odorata*)
Tobacco plant (*Nicotiana alata*)
Viburnum (*Viburnum* x *burkwoodii*)

AROMATIC PLANTS

Catmint (*Nepeta mussinii*)
Cotton lavender (*Santolina chamaecyparissus*)
Fennel (*Foeniculum vulgare*)
Pearl everlasting (*Anaphalis triplinervis*)
Purple sage (*Salvia officinalis* 'Purpurascens')
Rosemary (*Rosmarinus officinalis*)
Thyme (*Thymus* sp.)

Pearl Everlasting
(ANAPHALIS TRIPLINERVIS)

Catmint
(NEPETA MUSSINII)

FOLIAGE PLANTS FOR COLOUR

Silver-grey
Ballota (*Ballota* sp.)
Eucalyptus (*Eucalyptus* sp)
Hosta (*Hosta sieboldiana* var. *elegans*)
Lamb's tongue (*Stachys byzantina*)
Lavender (*Lavandula angustifolia*)
Old rose (*Rosa gallica*)
Rosemary (*Rosmarinus officinalis*)
Senecio (*Brachyglottis greyi*)
Wormwood (*Artemisia* sp.)

Purple
Heuchera (e.g. *Heuchera micrantha* 'Palace Purple')
Purple basil (*Ocimum basilicum*)
Purple sage (*Salvia officinalis* 'Purpurascens')

Variegated (yellow/green)
Dogwood (*Cornus alba* 'Elegantissima')
Euonymus (*Euonymus fortunei* 'Emerald 'n' Gold')
Holly (*Ilex aquifolium* 'Silver Queen')
Hosta (*Hosta fortunei* – various cultivars:
   H. sieboldiana 'Frances Williams')

Euonymus
(EUONYMUS FORTUNEI
'Emerald 'n' Gold')

Mimosa
(ACACIA DEALBATA)

Broom
(GENISTA sp.)

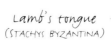

Lamb's tongue
(STACHYS BYZANTINA)

Purple sage
(SALVIA OFFICINALIS
'Purpurascens')

FLOWERS BY SEASON

Spring

Christmas rose (*Helleborus niger*,
  H. orientalis)
Dutch hyacinth (*Hyacinthus
  orientalis*)
Freesia (*Freesia* sp.)
Mimosa (*Acacia dealbata*)
Narcissus (*Narcissus* sp. – many)
Pansy (*Viola* sp.)
Polyanthus (*Primula* hybrid)
Scilla (*Scilla siberica*)
Snowdrops (*Galanthus* sp.)
Tulip (*Tulipa*)

Tulip
(TULIPA *sp.*)

Summer

Carnation/pink (*Dianthus* sp.)
Cornflower (*Centaurea cyanus*)
Gazania (*Gazania* sp.)
Gerbera (*Gerbera* sp.)
Lilac (*Syringa*)
Lily (*Lilium* sp. – many)
Ox-eye daises
   (*Leucanthemum* sp.)
Peony (*Paeonia* sp.)
Phlox (*Phlox* sp.)
Poppy (*Papaver* sp.)
Rose (*Rosa*)
Stock (*Matthiola*)

Lilac
(SYRINGA)

Autumn

Alder (*Alnus* sp.) – cones
Chinese lantern (*Physalis*)
Chrysanthemum (*Chrysanthemum* sp.)
Dahlia (*Dahlia*)
Firethorn (*Pyracantha* sp.) – berries
Golden rod (*Solidago* sp.)
Honesty (*Lunaria annua*) – seedheads
Ivy (*Hedera helix*) – berries
Rose (*Rosa*)
Yarrow (*Achillea millefolium*)

Ivy
(HEDERA *sp.*)

FLOWERS BY COLOUR

White flowers

Amaryllis (*Hippeastrum*)
Anthriscus (*Anthriscus sylvestris*)
Buttercup (*Ranunculus crenatus*,
  R. amplexicaulis)
Campion (*Silene fimbriata*)
Christmas rose (*Helleborus niger*)
Clematis (*Clematis* e.g. *C. armandii*,
  C. 'Wada's Primrose', *C. montana*)
Dutch hyacinth (*Hyacinthus orientalis*)
Eustoma (*Eustoma grandiflorum*)
Geranium (*Geranium phaeum* 'Album')
Gerbera (*Gerbera* sp.)
Gypsophila (*Gypsophila* sp.)
Hydrangea (*Hydrangea arborescens*)
Leptospermum (*Leptospermum* sp.)
Lilac (*Syringa vulgaris*)
Narcissus (e.g. *Narcissus* 'Pheasant's
  Eye', *N.* 'Paper White')
Night-scented stock (*Matthiola* sp.)
Regal lily (*Lilium regale*)
Rose (e.g. *Rosa rugosa* 'Alba', *R.* 'Iceberg')
Snapdragon (*Antirrhinum majus*)
Snowdrop (*Galanthus officinalis*)
Sweet pea (*Lathyrus odoratus*)
Tulip (*Tulipa*)

sweet pea
(LATHYRUS
ODORATA)

Yellow/orange

Alstroemeria (*Alstroemeria* sp.)
Buttercup (*Ranunculus* sp.)
Chrysanthemum (*Chrysanthemum* sp.)
Crocus (e.g. *Crocus angustifolius*,
  C. 'Golden Yellow')
Daylily (*Hemerocallis* sp.)
Euphorbia (*Euphorbia polychroma*)
Forsythia (*Forsythia* x *intermedia*)
Freesia (e.g. *Freesia* 'Rijnveld's Yellow',
  F. 'Yellow River')
Gerbera (*Gerbera*)
Lily (e.g. *Lilium* 'Connecticut King', *L.* 'Destiny')
Mimosa (*Acacia dealbata*)
Narcissus (e.g. *Narcissus* 'February Gold',
  N. 'Tête-à-Tête')
Poppy (e.g. *Papaver atlanticum*, *P. orientale*
  'May Queen')
Primula (e.g. *Primula aureata*, *P. auricula*)
Rudbeckia (*Rudbeckia* sp.)
Sunflower (*Helianthus* sp.)
Tulip (*Tulipa*)
Witch hazel (*Hamamelis mollis*)

Pink/red

Anemone (e.g. *Anemone blanda* 'Radar',
  A. x *fulgens*)
Camellia (*Camellia* sp.)
Columbine (*Aquilegia vulgaris*)
Gerbera (*Gerbera*)
Dutch hyacinth (e.g. *Hyacinthus orientalis*
  'Amsterdam' or 'Pink Pearl')
Heliconia (*Heliconia* sp.)
Lilac (e.g. *Syringa* 'Belle de Nancy',
  'Clarke's Giant')
Lisianthus (*Eustoma grandiflorum*)
Peony (*Paeonia* sp.)
Poppy (e.g. *Papaver commutatum* 'Ladybird',
  P. orientale 'Indian Chief')
Ranunculus (*Ranunculus asiaticus*)
Snapdragon (e.g. *Antirrhinum majus* 'Coronette'
  or 'His Excellency')
Sweet pea (*Lathyrus odorata*)
Tulip (*Tulipa*)

Anemone
(ANEMONE *sp.*)

Pansy
(VIOLA *sp.*)

Sunflower
(HELIANTHUS *sp.*)

Blue/Purple

Aconitum (*Aconitum* sp.)
Anemone (*Anemone* sp.)
Bluebell (*Hyacinthoides non-scripta*)
Brunnera (*Brunnera macrophylla*)
Catmint (*Nepeta* x *fassennii*)
Clematis (e.g. *Clematis* 'Daniel
  Deronda', *C.* 'Jackmanii')
Delphinium (e.g. *Delphinium* x
  belladonna, *D. elatum* 'Fenella')
Dutch hyacinth (e.g. *Hyacinthus orientalis*
  'Blue Jacket' or 'Ostara')
Iris (e.g. *Iris* 'Dreaming Spires',
  I. latifolia 'Blue Giant')
Pansy (*Viola* x *wittrockiana*)
Polyanthus (*Primula* hybrid)
Sweet Pea (*Lathyrus odorata*)

Delphinium
(DELPHINIUM
X BELLADONNA)

ACKNOWLEDGEMENTS

Jenny Raworth and **Susan Berry** would like to thank the following people for all their hard work in helping to create this book: **Mike Newton**, assisted by **Richard Smith**, for his excellent photography; **Debbie Mole** for art directing and designing the book; **Leeann Mackenzie** for help with the styling; **Gabrielle Townsend** and the team at *Phoebus Editions* for all their hard work putting the book together; **Catharina Mannerfelt**, **Mike Newton** and **Irena Hamilton**

for allowing us to photograph in their homes, and **Catharina** also for lending props from her shop, **The Blu Door**, *74 Church Road, Barnes, London SW13 0DQ, tel 0181 748 9745;* **Broadway Florists**, *155 Heath Road Twickenham, Middlesex, TW1 4BH, tel. 0181 892 5774* and the **Conservatory Flower Shop**, *13 Brewers Lane Richmond, Surrey TW9 1HH, tel. 0181 940 2265, fo* supplying so many of the flowers.